Center for International Studies
Massachusetts Institute of Technology
Cambridge, Massachusetts

STUDIES OF THE PROGRAM IN INTERNATIONAL COMMUNICATION

1. *La Querelle de la CED,* Raymond Aron and Daniel Lerner, eds. Librairie Armand Colin, Paris, 1956. *The Defeat of EDC,* Daniel Lerner and Raymond Aron, eds. Frederick A. Praeger, New York, 1957.

2. *Elite Communication in Samoa,* by Felix and Marie Keesing, Stanford University Press, 1956.

3. *Studies in Political Communication,* special issue *Public Opinion Quarterly,* Spring 1956, Ithiel de Sola Pool, ed.

4. *Japanese Popular Culture,* Hidetoshi Kato, ed. Charles E. Tuttle Co., Rutland, Vt. and Tokyo, Japan, 1959.

5. *Modernizing the Middle East, Studies in Communication and Social Change,* by Daniel Lerner.

6. *Changing Images of America, A Study of Indian and Social Change,* by Daniel Lerner, The Free Press, Glencoe, Ill., 1958.

7. *Scratches on Our Minds, American Images of India and China,* by Harold Isaacs, John Day, New York, 1958.

JAPANESE POPULAR CULTURE

JAPANESE POPULAR CULTURE

Edited and Translated by
Hidetoshi Kato

Studies in Mass Communication and
Cultural Change

Made at the
Institute of Science of Thought, Japan

CHARLES E. TUTTLE COMPANY

Rutland, Vt., Tokyo, Japan

Published by the
Charles E. Tuttle Company
of Rutland, Vermont & Tokyo, Japan
with editorial offices at
15 Edogawa-cho, Bunkyo-ku, Tokyo

Library of Congress Catalog Card
No. 58-5088

First edition, 1959

Book design and typography by
Roland A. Mulhauser

Printed in Japan by the
Tokyo News Service, Ltd.

CONTENTS

7

FOREWORD

The culture of Japan has long intrigued the West. We
have been charmed by beautiful prints, scrolls, dancers,
costumes, and objects of everyday use. On Japanese fine
and minor arts there is a vast literature in English. Particularly since the War, many Americans have come to know
and be interested in things Japanese. But when one culture
is thus introduced to another culture, that which is introduced is apt to be high-brow culture. In Japan as elsewhere
some gulf exists between the creative art of the sophisticates
and the popular arts which flow through the mass media.
It follows that in the process of international communication the material which is not "worthy" of being translated
gets lost from view and is unknown abroad. With the
exception of the Hollywood motion picture, it is hard to
think of an instance in which those cultural products of a
country which are actually its most characteristic and
widely diffused ones are also the ones by which foreigners
know it. Comic strips, popular songs, cheap periodicals
pass unnoticed and unrecorded by those who chronicle the
ways of the world.

From the point of view of the artist or the educator, this
is perhaps as it should be, but for the student of human
behavior the dross is data as much as the pure gold. We
can perhaps learn even more of the dreams and myths of
a people from their daily fare of pot boiler than from the

9

universal achievements of their most rarefied minds. For the student of society, therefore, the process of selective winnowing of what is translated is a source of frustration and misperception. The many books about Japanese fine arts or the translations of first-rate Japanese literature published in the United States are of course valuable means toward international cultural understanding. But they are not an adequate clue for an American reader who is interested in the life of the common people in contemporary Japan. For that we need other evidence.

American social scientists have been aware for some time of vigorous activity among Japanese students of public opinion and communications and of the fact that in Japanese there existed important descriptions of contemporary social life. Almost every Japanese newspaper has used public opinion polls and audience surveys. The study of the mass media and popular culture is also highly developed, but to most American social scientists what has been done in Japan has been a closed book. A few Japanese-speaking scholars have brought word back to us of the studies of the Institute of Science of Thought and other groups. In 1953 in the *Far Eastern Quarterly* R. P. Dore presented a survey of the work of the Institute with some tantalizing sketches of a few research results. Other sources have conveyed bits of information from time to time. The Center for Japanese Studies at Ann Arbor published an occasional paper by Joseph K. Yamagiwa on *Regional Differences in Literary Tastes and Reputations in Japan*. But these scattered reports in English were just sufficient to convince us of the importance of the studies which we could not read.

It was for this reason that the Center for International Studies at MIT, which is engaged in a research program on international communication, was pleased to make contact with Mr. Hidetoshi Kato, the author of some studies of popular culture in Japan. He was in Cambridge as a visiting Rockefeller Foundation Fellow in 1954-55. We asked

him if he would select a representative group of the more
interesting studies and translate them. This he has done,
and we are now offering them to the English-speaking
reader.

Of the common threads which run through the studies,
one deserves particular note. That thread deals with the
profound change in traditional Japanese culture and values
under the impact of the development of the mass media and
of intercultural contact particularly during the Occupation.
Whether it be in norms as to the desirable shape for a
woman's bosom, or in the names of bars and taverns, or in
the breakdown of familial relationships, the impact of the
Occupation on popular culture is unmistakable in these
essays. Of course, the articles here presented were written
in the postwar years of enforced and dramatic change.
Those who know Japan today might find them already a
bit out of date. In some respects one might observe a
reaction at the moment; in other respects one would see the
continuing march of the new. But the long-run trend away
from the life of a traditional society to that of a modern
cosmopolitan one is beyond dispute. Even had there been
no war and no Occupation, the mass media, perhaps more
slowly, would have played their role as agents of this epoch-
making change.

No aspect of this change is more stressed in the stories
herein analyzed than the conflict between the norms and
controls of the traditional family and the modern aspirations of the younger generation. These familiar conflicts
focus on sex, career aspirations, and the role of women.
The heroes are often radical and nihilistic, the heroines
victims of outmoded customs. The outcomes are varied.
Sometimes the ways of the future triumph; sometimes the
wisdom of the old is recognized and the rebel returns, at
least in part, to the values of his fathers. Whatever the
details of the treatment, the theme is a familiar one and
universal to the process of modernization which the mass
media entail. It is a central theme not only in this volume,

11

but also in many of the other volumes of the Center for International Studies series of which this one is a part. It is the focus of Mr. Lerner's study of modernization in the Middle East; it turns up in the Keesings' study of communications in Samoa, and again in the Center studies in India. The mass media, even in their most unenlightened forms open up new vistas and new world views. The contents of popular writings and dramas may not be enlightened, but the imaginary population of characters they present includes peoples of types far beyond the first hand ken of the peasant or housewife who may listen to them. It is easy to be contemptuous of popular culture, it is important also to recognize its broadening social role. Scholars were shocked and often unbelieving when they learned from Hertha Herzog's classic study of the American radio soap opera that one of its strong holds on its listeners was that they found it educational. The listeners were right. They were gaining from it acquaintance with sectors of the world that they could never know at first hand and also reinforcement and guidance of their groping impulses towards a value system into which they could fit the experiences that a fluid modern world thrust on them. The same sort of thing happens in Japan. The mass media are an agent of change and modernity.

The sympathies of the Japanese social scientists who write about this cultural revolution are clearly on the side of the new as against the old. In many of the articles to follow there are moralistic conclusions drawn, to the effect that popular culture cannot become really good until it assumes crusading responsibilities on the side of progress. The words "progress" and "progressive" are often used by our authors with the slightly magical overtones with which we are familiar from other countries (both communist and democratic) where the great issue is that of modernization. The Marxist world myth obviously gives expression to this craving for the destruction of the "feudal" past and the achieving of an equalitarian and industrialized future.

12

Whether in Marxist or non-Marxist versions the overtones of this ideological bias against Japan's "feudal" heritage and in favor of social change form a common thread in most Japanese studies of Japanese society or culture.

In order to set the following articles in a context which would make them more meaningful to American readers we asked Mr. Herbert Passin, a leading American student of Japan, to give us an overview of the amount, types, and conditions of production of current writing in Japan. This he has done in the Preface. We also asked Mr. Kato to add a factual appendix on the dissemination of the mass media.

There are many persons without whose cooperation this book would not have been possible and to whom we wish to express our gratitude. First among them are the several authors who permitted the use of their articles. The essays in the body of the book were all written by members of the Institute of Science of Thought, which published them originally in Japanese. We are grateful to the Institute for its cooperation in the preparation of the book. Thanks are also due to the Dentsu Advertising Agency, the Institute of Social Psychology, and two newspapers, the *Asahi,* and the *Mainichi,* for their cooperation in the assembling of statistical materials and their permission to use them. Mrs. Takae Kato cooperated with Mr. Kato in the preparation of the translations. During the Katos' stay in this country David Riesman was particularly helpful in encouraging this project. Miss Martha Tucker and Mrs. Elizabeth Colt helped in the final editing of the translations. To all these people and to others too numerous to mention, we wish to express our thanks and acknowledgement.

ITHIEL DE SOLA POOL
Center for International Studies, M.I.T.

PREFACE[1]

by Herbert Passin

It may seem strange on first sight to introduce a book on the "mass society" with a discussion of intellectuals, writers, and magazines. We automatically make a disjunction in our minds between the "intellectuals" and the "masses", and it is undeniably true that in many contexts this is an important one. But seen from a larger point of view, the intellectuals are just as much a distinctive feature of mass society as are the modern masses themselves.

If we compare feudal Japan with Japan of the Riesmannian age, this point will be clear. Before her entry into the modern world in 1868, Japanese society was characterized by the social and class types that pertain to a feudal society: nobility, warriors, peasants, merchants, and even outcastes. Intellectual life was carried on by clerics, by leisured members of the warrior and noble classes, and by occasional inspired individuals from the merchant class. Today, however, the spectrum of social life is entirely different, not unlike what we are familiar with in Western Europe and America: capitalists, managers, bankers, journalists, specialists in the mass media, skilled workers, unskilled workers, rich farmers, poor farmers, students, artists, and intellectuals. The intellectual is as organic

---

1. This article is slightly adapted from one that has appeared in *Encounter* (England) under the title "A Nation of Readers—and of Writers, Too", March 1957, pp. 33-37.

a part of the scene as are the masses—the workers, the peasants, and the lower-middle classes.

Without entering the tricky terrain of defining what an intellectual is or how many there are, we can say, on an informed common-sense basis, that the hosts of journalists, artists, teachers, academic personnel, university students, engineers, writers, higher civil servants, and scientists—that is, of people whose lives and livelihood are bound up in some way with intellectual production—must run into the millions. At the present time there are somewhere in the neighborhood of 600,000 university students scattered in somewhat over 500 universities and colleges throughout the country. This enormous mass forms part of the very definition of modern life—or to be more precise, of the most recent phase of modern life, the "mass society"—in exactly the same sense as the radio, movies, television, comic strips, and spectatorship at baseball games.

The discussion which follows, therefore, deals with an important aspect of modern life in Japan. If it is not the life of the "shomin"—the common people, the masses—it is still a thing of large numbers of people, great influence on the intellectual and political life of the country, large-scale production, mass impact, and even of big business. It is a brief glimpse into one aspect of the life of the "educated masses". Just as we cannot form a correct picture of Japan only from Mt. Fuji, cherry blossoms, geisha, and samurai—important though these things be—so we would be off base to think of Japan only in terms of the workers, peasants, and lower middle classes.

*   *   *

The famous woman writer looked around slowly at the appointments of the Western-style restaurant to which I had taken her for dinner, her sllghly dazed eyes clearing gradually as if she were coming up from some great depth. "I've been so busy," she said, "that I scarcely have time for anything. I have to eat lunch literally with chopsticks

16

in my left hand and pen in my right." But this is no
exceptional story among Japanese writers. My friend is
certainly busier than most, but there are probably more
people in Japan classifiable as "writers," who make all
or most of their living from writing—rather than from
teaching, lecturing, journalism, or business—than in any
other country in the world. The demand is so great that,
in a quite literal sense, physical endurance becomes a significant factor in the writer's income. As far as sheer
volume is concerned, there are several important writers
who have already outstripped Balzac—and some of them
have many years of creative work still lying ahead of them.

Nor does all this work go unrecognised and unrewarded.
Writers rank high in the income tax lists (only because
they cannot conceal their incomes like doctors and other
professionals, some would complain). Like movie actors,
they have a high ratio of automobile ownership, although
the general pattern in Japan is to use the "company car,"
rather than own one's own. My friend apologised to me
for not having an automobile by explaining that she was
too busy to take time out for going down, selecting a car,
purchasing it, registering it, insuring it, finding a chauf-
feur, etc. . . . .

If you ask people to explain this tremendous pressure,
they will tell you that it is not because there are only a few
writers, as might be the case in some South-East Asian
countries. A recent estimate listed more than 1,000 professional free-lance writers, earning all or most of their
income from writing. The almost standard explanation is:
"We are a nation of readers. The people are so poor here
that they cannot afford other amusements and so they go
in for reading." Like the familiar argument about the
birthrate being high in backward rural areas because there
is no electric light and people have nothing else to do at
night, this is only part of the truth. There are other peoples
besides the Japanese who find money short and time hanging heavy on their hands, but they do not necessarily go

17

in for reading. Furthermore, it should follow from this argument that the amount of reading goes down as Japan becomes more prosperous. And this, as anyone can plainly see, is not so. The amount of reading in Japan, as measured by annual sales of all kinds of published matter, goes up year by year. Japan has the most flourishing publishing industry in the world, if not in terms of business profits, then certainly in the production of words *per capita*. Japanese writers themselves in their more candid moments refer to it as a "verbal diarrhoea," and it takes many writers to keep the stream of words flowing through all the magazines, newspapers, books, radios, television sets, movies, and theatres.

One needs no more than a short ride on public transportation to realise this. Even General MacArthur, who rarely left his eagle's nest in the Dai-Ichi Insurance Building in downtown Tokyo to survey his realm, was augustly impressed by the sight of students reading books and magazines off the racks in the mile-long row of bookshops lining the Jimbo-cho district of Tokyo. "The future lies with these young people," he pontificated, puffing on his corncob pipe. The magazine has become as standard a part of the scene as the white-collar worker's brief-case, or the high-school student's black and slightly shiny uniform, or the tired housewife's cloth-wrapped parcel. When the train lurches, you are as likely as not to receive a magazine full in the face from your swaying neighbour, too intent on his article to notice your presence.

Social psychologists have commented that the pace of life in the United States is bringing into existence a new type of magazine, small, compact, swiftly readable, one that allows the eye to glide over it with a minimal engagement of the mind. If this be a reasonable explanation for the Quickies, the Peekies, and the Five-Minute Novels, which can be read on subways, at traffic stops while waiting for the signal to change, or shooting up to the sixtieth floor in a lift, then we must conclude that Japan is still a slow-motion country. Or that the average Japanese commuter's ride is so much longer than the American's that he needs a much larger magazine to fill in the time. A quick survey among my friends reveals that commuting up to three hours per day—one to one-and-a-half hours each way—is not uncommon. The added reading time that this permits has resulted in the development of a magazine of such heft that the ordinary reader in other countries would hesitate even to lift it up. I have before me an array of monthly magazines, all of a fairly "serious" type. The American *Atlantic Monthly* runs 122 pages; *Encounter* about 88; *Twentieth Century* about 84—while the issue I have in hand of the Japanese *Chuo Koron,* which is if anything more "serious" than these, runs to 374 pages!

All of this suggests a weightiness that is confirmed by figures. There are almost 1,300 different magazines published in Japan, with an annual total of about 360 million copies. Every month the National Railways carry about 14,300 tons of magazines in almost eight hundred freight-cars. If to this we add the 3,000 tons carried by trucks and estimate about 3,000 tons as the weight of magazines delivered within Tokyo, then we get a total delivered weight of about 20,000 tons of magazines per month. Dividing by the over-32 million individual numbers published, and making allowance for the weight of wrapping materials used in delivery, we get an average startlingly like one pound per copy.

Since at this very moment I am holding in my hand a thin magazine of no more than three ounces, I dread to think what this average of one pound implies at the other end. But let us stay with statistics another moment. At 32 million copies per month, or between 360 and 400 million per year, we get an average of almost two magazines per month per family, or about 24 per year. Now by any standards this is a large readership. And if to this we add a 34 million daily newspaper circulation, or 2.2 newspapers per family, and an average of more than 130 million books published per year, or about eight per family, we cannot escape the conclusion that Japanese people spend a good part of their time reading—to put it mildly. One must sympathise with the 10th-century Emperor who was so astonished that his people should be able to read such vast quantities of poetry. The official anthology of twenty chapters was far too much, he complained. "I am sure for my part," said the Emperor, according to Sei Shonagon, the great diarist, "I shall never succeed in getting beyond Chapter Two."

It is no surprise that in any literate modern nation, magazines angled for a mass audience—light fiction, true stories, movie magazines, sports magazines, housewives' magazines, etc.—have large circulations. And Japan is no exception. A magazine with the singularly infelicitous title, one would think, of *Heibon,* which means "mediocrity," or "run-of-the-mill," or "ordinary," has the largest monthly circulation in the country, about 1.4 million. Similarly the *Ie no Hikari* ("Light of the Home"), a farm family magazine, runs over 1 million. Even the translated Japanese edition of the *Reader's Digest* finds 400,000 buyers. What is surprising is the extent to which serious writers are published in the popular magazines. One could not say that there is no distinction at all between popular and highbrow writers, but it certainly has much less significance here than in the West. "Good" writers appear with great frequency in the large mass-circulated magazines, not only in the elevated intellectual journals.

But what makes Japan distinctive above all is the vigour of its intellectual journalism. Serious magazines can be a commercially sound proposition. If we take as a rough working definition of "serious" those magazines that deal with ideas, literature, political analysis, art, etc., we shall find *several hundred* of all descriptions. To take a few random examples, there are seventeen "general magazines," almost sixty strictly literary magazines, twenty that concentrate on modern poetry, forty-eight given over to the tradi-

tional 31-syllable Japanese poem (the *tanka*), and fifty-one
to the 17-syllable *haiku*—even the exotic *senryu* has eight.
Their aggregate circulation must be somewhere in the neigh-
bourhood of 10 per cent of the entire flow of periodical
literature, and if the weeklies and children's magazines be
excluded, almost 20 per cent. The single class of "general
magazines," which corresponds in level approximately to the
Atlantic Monthly, Harper's, Encounter, and so on, is 5 per
cent of the total national magazine circulation; but in Tokyo, which is the cultural centre of the country, it outstrips
the "popular entertainment" magazines 26 per cent to 20
per cent, and if we were to consider the monthly adult
magazines alone, the proportion in Tokyo would be even
more impressive.

The big three, the heavyweights of the "general magazine" world, are *Bungei Shunju* ("Literary Journal"), with
a circulation of about 50,000; *Sekai* ("World") about
120,000; and *Chuo Koron* ("Central Review"), about 110,-
000. (These are only rough estimates; circulation figures
are closely guarded business, and even political, secrets).
For the really relentless intellectual, *Bungei Shunju* is practically a "popular magazine." In order to understand just
what this implies as to the snobbishness of Japanese readers, let us look at the contents of a typical issue. There
were twenty-six major items—articles, stories, symposia—
plus a dozen or more short items. Fifty or more writers
can open its pages and find their bylines. We find such
articles as "On the Spirit of Modern Escapism" by Professor
Nakaya, the distinguished low-temperature physicist and
the world's greatest authority on snow and ice crystals, who
is also in constant demand as a writer and commentator;
"Diplomacy, the Foreign Office, and Diplomats" by the late
Professor Otaka, of the Law Faculty of Tokyo University; a
symposium on the new course of Soviet politics participated
in by a distinguished professor of economics, a Soviet specialist, and the Director of the International House; "The
Relations of the Social and the Natural Sciences" by Profes-

sor Tsuru, the distinguished economist; "Ricardo's Travel Record" by Dr. Koizumi, the former President of Keio University and now in charge of the Crown Prince's education; and so on. Certainly no lack of weight here. The explanation for its "unseriousness" in the eyes of some is partly that *Bungei Shunju* does not go along completely with the fashionable leftism of intellectual circles and partly that it makes a deliberate effort at readability. All of *Bungei Shunju's* writers are serious, but they write here in their somewhat less Teutonic and academic vein.

It is at the next level upward that we come to the standard fare of Japanese intellectuals and students. *Sekai* is a postwar magazine, now in its eleventh year, supported by the powerful Iwanami Publishing House. In October 1951, after several years of modest existence, it hit the jackpot with a special issue attacking the San Francisco peace treaty, and shot up from somewhat under 10,000 to its present figure, which varies between 100,000 and 200,000. *Chuo Koron,* now in its seventy-second year of publication, has a distinguished history in the intellectual life of modern Japan. In general it tries to steer a roughly non-partisan course, but since it is a magazine of, by, and for Japanese intellectuals, it cannot avoid inclining toward their dominant mood of the moment. It has therefore not always been distinguishable politically from *Sekai.*

A third member of this charmed circle, *Kaizo* ("Reconstruction"), with a circulation of about 70,000, and even more strenuously intellectual than the others, recently failed after thirty-five years of publication. The gap has been filled with an alarming alacrity, some of the readers having gone to other general magazines—*Chuo Koron,* for example, experienced a slight increase in circulation—and others, more ominously, to the fast-growing weeklies, which are taking on more and more the character of "general magazines," except that they are smaller, more readable, and cheaper. (*Chuo Koron* costs 150 yen, or about $.42 but a weekly costs only $.10.)

If we compare the Japanese general magazines with their counterparts in other countries, we are first struck by their enormous range. One wonders how anyone can find time to read them. And a little enquiry will turn up the shame-faced admission that many people buy them so as not to seem "non-intellectual," but do not really read them. Taking a magazine, particularly a serious magazine, is frequently an act of identification rather than a mere choice of reading matter. Many functions that we are accustomed to see divided among different types of magazines will be found together here. There is something for every taste. They seem to be simultaneously literary magazines, journals of political comment, and news reviews. They carry fiction, biography, essays, reportage, economic analyses, literary criticism, music and art criticism, symposia, and philosophical articles.

They also seem to feel it necessary to be up-to-the-minute in their news and political comment. Therefore political and economic writers are often called upon to knock out a piece at a few hours' notice. In urgent cases, the writer is locked away in a hotel room—if he is well known, his "prison" may be some elegant Japanese-style inn with hot spring baths and tempting foods—and messengers stand by, sometimes in relays, to rush each precious page as it is completed to the printers. There is no question that in this way a genuine topicality is attained, but it is often at the expense of sloppy writing. Thus the monthlies show, instead of the quiet, reflective remoteness that we associate with them in the West, much of the tension and sensitivity of the daily newspaper office.

This jittery responsiveness to current events as well as the bitter competition among the magazines has brought on a race every month to see who can hit the streets first. Most magazines reach the stands a good two weeks before their face date. Thus the April issue of most magazines is already sold by March 15th. *Sekai* appears on the 7th of the month preceding its date of publication. But the *reductio ad absurdum* of this system is *Myojo* ("Morning Star") which appears forty-five days in advance!—its July issue appears on the stands on May 15th.

Magazine economics, even in the case of the highbrow magazines, is very complex. Most important magazines are now firmly embraced within some sizeable enterprise. The Big Three newspapers operate chains of magazines, both monthlies and weeklies, as a kind of staff overflow from their regular operations, appealing to different levels of the population from elementary school pupils to intellectuals. But for some reason, the upper end of the scale has not worked out, and their "general magazines" have all failed.

The powerful publishing houses have been more successful at this level. The Iwanami House, for example, the main puplisher of academic works, has a whole string of intellectual and academic journals—their stable includes eleven serious magazines (like "Scientific Research," "Economic Research," "Biological Science," and "Agricultural Economics Research") with the general magazine *Sekai* as its front-runner. The more popular Kodansha Company works the other end of the range, with magazines for children, boys, girls, adolescents, women, etc.; however, even Kodansha feels it necessary to maintain a "general magazine" for purposes of prestige, though it loses money. The Shincho Company, which publishes the second largest number of book titles per year in Japan (almost nine hundred), maintains a string of highbrow magazines, topped by the "general magazine" *Shincho*.

All of this, as one might suspect, adds up to a paradise for the writer, even though many of them, without knowledge of conditions elsewhere, complain loudly all the time. Writers—by which I mean both the full-time professionals and the hosts of professors, diplomats, artists, and even businessmen who earn a measurable proportion of their income from writing — are called upon constantly for articles not only on their own specialities, where they may be presumed to have something to say, but also on matters

24

very distant indeed. It is therefore not uncommon to find a professor of philosophy writing on the latest turn in Japanese-Soviet negotiations over fishery, or to hear the measured comments of an adventure-story writer on the promotion of trade with South-East Asia. It cannot be denied that all of this adds a certain freshness and liveliness to Japanese journalism. And it does break down some of the traditional ivory tower isolation of the universities, keeping the scholars in touch with the public and its problems, and the public familiar with scholarly names. A survey several years back, for example, found that of the ten most popular writers among young people, three were professors; and that three of the ten largest contributors in the magazines (judged by the number of printed words in a sample period) were professors. But one cannot remark with equal confidence that this frenetic pace is good for the quality of the writing. The magazines are, of course, only one station on a busy round—which includes the newspapers, weeklies and the radio as well. Writers are so busy filling the varied requests of the journals that they simply lack the time to read, to study, to write carefully, to reflect on their arguments. And in the universities, one often hears from students as well as from less fortunate faculty members the complaint that the "glamour boys," the popular writing-professors, neglect the preparation of their courses and lectures.

Another disturbing feature is that most writing is done on direct commission. The journal decides the subject and then commissions someone to write on it. In the case of my woman writer friend, for example, she has in the past year written three novels—two serialised in magazines, one in a daily newspaper—four short stories, twenty essays and journalistic pieces on political, social, feministic, literary, and international matters, plus about eighty weekly columns in the newspapers—all on direct request. This is in addition to a full programme of radio appearances, round-table discussions, and lectures. It is a long time since she has had the leisure to sit down to write simply because there was something she particularly wanted to write.

This would still not be so bad if one could be sure that the reader is as well served as the writer. To be sure, he is treated to an enormous range of subjects, a reasonably good coverage of world events, and a tremendous variety of creative literature. But does he get a balanced range of political views? The answer is, regrettably, no. As the English poet D. J. Enright noticed during his stay in Japan, "conservatives govern the country, but socialists govern the bookshops." In certain journals, what might be called the "pre-Khrushchev anti-Stalinist" hasn't a chance. The writer who is too out-spoken in his expression of non-standard political views will find that he runs the danger of being excluded from certain publishing outlets. Not from all, to be sure, but from enough to affect his earning capacity. Therefore many writers will carefully steer clear of subjects that might bring them afoul of prevailing editorial sentiment and brand them as "reactionaries"—the dreadest curse word among Japanese intellectuals—and cut off the flow of requests they need for making a living; or they will in the worst cases deliberately misstate their true views. The result is an appearance of political uniformity in the main serious journals that is not only misleading but harmful. Editors, writers, and readers are all caught up in the vicious circle. The writer writes in a certain way to be sure that he will continue to be published; the editor biases his selections because he feels that this is what his readers want (a conscientious editor does not even have to suppress nonconformist writers; all he has to do is to assign them to "safe" topics); and the reader feels that this is the weight of intelligent opinion because the best-known writers say it in the best-known journals.

But perhaps all of this is to be laid to the *Zeitgeist*, the political conditions of our times. If one can set these criticisms apart, then the Japanese serious magazines are probably—and from the standpoint of the writer, certainly—the liveliest and most successful in the world.

THE AUTHORS

KENICHI ADACHI, former chief editor of the newspaper *Shinosaka*. Now with the weekly magazine *Shyukan-shincho*, and the *Nippon Sendensha* advertising agency.

KANJI HATANO, Professor of Educational Psychology, Ochanomizu Women's University, Tokyo.

TAIHEI IMAMURA, film critic, regular contributor of criticisms to the Jiji news service.

HIDETOSHI KATO, Institute of Humanistic Sciences, Kyoto University; formerly Rockefeller Fellow at Harvard University and University of Chicago.

HIROSHI MINAMI, Assistant Professor of Social Psychology, Hitotsubashi University, Tokyo. Dean, Institute of Social Psychology, his private research organization.

MAMORU MOCHIZUKI, Professor of Psychology, Chiba University.

TADATOSHI OKUBU, linguistic psychologist, author and translator of books in general semantics and linguistics.

TSUTOMU ONO, farmer.

MICHITARO TADA, Research Associate, Institute of Humanistic Science, Kyoto University. Specialist on French literature and general theory of aesthetics.

SHUNSUKE TSURUMI, Assistant Professor of Philosophy, Tokyo Institute of Technology.

THE DEVELOPMENT OF COMMUNICATION RESEARCH IN JAPAN

by Hidetoshi Kato

During and before the war, it was a characteristic of the Japanese army and navy that they did not use the common Japanese language. Instead they adopted the literary language of which even the grammatical construction is different from the colloquial. Soldiers, therefore, had great difficulty in reading army documents. The *Emperor's Words to the Armed Forces* and many other army textbooks were written in the literary language employing difficult Chinese characters which average primary school graduates, and even high school graduates, could not read and understand.

This inconvenient and inefficient system led to mal-communication between the army and the people. To a student of communication, this army communication system suggests problems which Japanese communication habits in general share. Let us say a few words about the characteristics of Japanese communication before we begin a discussion of the history of Japanese communication research.

I. MAJOR CHARACTERISTICS OF JAPANESE COMMUNICATION

1) Plurality of Communication Systems:

Mr. Shunsuke Tsurumi has pointed out that there have been at least two completely different communication systems (and ways of thinking) in Japanese society. One is a very formal mode of communication which all people "ought to use," and the other is the people's own device. The former, which is represented by *The Imperial Rescript on Education*,* is composed of stereotypic words and expressions devised by bureaucrats and indoctrinated into the people in order to "educate" them. The latter, according to Mr. Tsurumi, is represented in *Iroha Karuta* (a set of playing cards on each of which is written a popular proverb), which is the product of the people's experience and wisdom.

The former, which most people could recite but without understanding the meaning, was a ritualistic communication. For a high school entrance examination before the war, such topics as "Japan in the World" or "The Way of the Sacred People" were frequently set as subjects of a composition. This examination was, in fact, a test to measure how skillfully a student used stereotypic words. An adult Japanese expressed his opinion in public only through the government approved words.

In Mr. Tsurumi's words, "The stereotypic phrasings disseminated by the government became a factor which defined even people's daily conversation."

---

* *Kyoiku Chokugo*—was given by the late Emperor Meiji in 1890. The content is the principles which people should obey. Even primary school pupils were supposed to recite the whole statement, so that it would be a bible of Japanese national morale.

While this bureaucratic culture was formalistic and rigid, the common man's culture behind the scenes developed its own flexible syntax though it could not be used in public.

The plurality of communication systems opens up many interesting and difficult problems. For example, there developed a clear schism between the elite's and the people's way of thinking. Intellectuals and the masses could not understand each other, partly because they lived in quite different communication circles.

2) Ambiguity:

In the Japanese language, emotional and suggestive attributes are very strong. As Mr. Imamura points out in his article on Japanese movies, even the distinction between "Yes" and "No" is sometimes ambiguous, unless the listener carefully watches the speaker's gestures and facial expression.

An important subject is often communicated at a pre-verbal level. In traditional arts the essential point was taught by the "mind to mind" method. In the Zen school of Buddhism, sometimes communication is done without words. Two priests facing each other without talking may mean that they are talking by eyes and minds.

Another ambiguity is found in metaphorical expressions. In Mr. Imamura's article, as well as in Mr. Minami's study of popular songs, it is emphasized that people prefer to express their emotion through the metaphor of "natural objects." A "foggy night" means "sadness," a butterfly may mean "hope." If I may exaggerate, sometimes Japanese communication is like the Rorschach method, that is, a communicatee should grasp a specific meaning from the ambiguous description of the communicator, but unlike Rorschach there is supposed to be only one correct meaning in the ambiguity.

3) Formalism:

Weston La Barre was right in his observation of Japanese character insofar as he said, "Japanese ceremoniousness is even expressed in the varying grades of honorific language, which differ not only in vocabulary but also in grammar itself."*

There are a handful of second person pronouns in Japanese among which a particular one should be carefully selected according to the situation in which the communication takes place. Verbs and auxiliary verbs should be replaced by the appropriate ones depending on to whom one is speaking. Failure in the choice of correct words may mean impoliteness. Proper word selection for a given interpersonal situation is, in fact, a very troublesome thing. Consequently, the people are more conscious about the *form* of communication than about the *content*.

This formalism, plus stereotypic communication, produces "hidden emotion." A person may not say what he wants to say because it may be impolite and dangerous. Mere tabulations of responses to a public opinion poll in Japan, therefore, do not reflect what people are really thinking.

4) Closed Communication:

Miss Kazuko Tsurumi defined Japanese communication as a "closed communication" by which she meant that in Japan, a communication is apt to become intrapersonal rather than interpersonal. People are not aware of how strong opinions are on national and international politics, even in their own small groups. The part of their communication which they cannot express in interpersonal situations is internalized and becomes "self conversation."

---

* Weston La Barre, "Some Observations on Character Structure in the Orient; The Japanese," *Psychiatry,* Vol. VIII, No. 3 (1945), p. 326.

In my opinion, this intrapersonal pattern of communication is the result of a semi-feudalistic social structure in which people did not have freedom of speech, and where silence was golden.*

5) *Magical Use of Words:*

"Magic of language" is a rather universal phenomenon. But in my opinion, Japan is the country where this magic is stronger than in other highly mechanized nations.

Above we discussed the Imperial Rescripts. These stereotypic expressions were, in fact, used magically. When a problem is settled in terms of these stereotypic words, it becomes an absolute postulate instead of a problem. Such terms as "for the Emperor," "for the Sacred Nation" were absolute and no one could doubt or even discuss them. Consequently, some officially approved words became amulets rather than conveyers of meanings.

This magical response to symbols may partly be due to the fact that in Shintoist doctrine (Shintoism is the only national religion which justifies the Emperor system), the animistic view of language was dominant. During the war, even among university professors, Koto Dama (spirit of language) was seriously discussed.

Another form of magic takes place in mass persuasion. Since the Japanese people have been ruled by authoritarian governments for a considerable period, they are still apt to believe everything communicated in the name of authority, especially by the bureaucrats.

---

* Two Japanese proverbs are good illustrations.

"Don't let them know, but let them rely" was the concise political philosophy of the feudal lords, and this policy was adopted by the Emperor's government until 1945.

"I will not see, hear, talk" is a popular proverb. This principle has been the least dangerous way of living. This attitude, at present, is taking the form of political apathy and cynicism.

In the field of mass communication, major newspapers and radio stations were very closely connected with the governmental authorities. Until 1946, the only radio network was N.H.K. or Japanese Broadcasting Association, which was managed on a semi-governmental level. It reflected the government's opinion rather than people's public opinion. The people believed the content of mass media because they were the agents of the government.

II. HISTORY OF COMMUNICATION STUDIES IN JAPAN

These characteristics of Japanese communication prevented not only communication itself but also the study of communication problems. In the prewar period, the study of communication did not develop because: (1) Where there is no freedom of speech, there is no freedom also for the study of speech, (2) Sociologists and psychologists were busy introducing theoretical developments from abroad instead of empirically studying Japanese society. Ivory tower intellectualism was an obstacle.

In the prewar period, however, such scholars as Ikutaro Shimizu, Jun Tosaka, and Kiyoshi Miki, did publish several articles on journalism. These are all rather moralistic and critical and lack empirical data.

Hence, in a strict sense, communication research in Japan started only several years ago. Even the term "communication" is, for the lack of proper translation, being used as an English lexical borrowing.

All aspects of Japanese culture, including the academic disciplines, were considerably Americanized in the postwar period. Japanese scholars became interested in communication under the influence of American sociology. The initiative for the study of communication problems was taken by a group of scholars called The Institute of

Science of Thought (hereafter abbreviated as IST). It was originally composed of young scholars including some who studied in the United States during the war. Their interest was the study of Japanese culture through behavioral sciences in the American sense. According to Mr. R. P. Dore,* one of the foreign scholars interested in IST, the characteristics of this group are: (1) that they are very conscious of the role of intellectuals in Japanese society, (2) that they are interested in studying the philosophy of the common man.

Many valuable studies have been made by this group during the past few years, including: (a) a series on the philosophy of the common man based on interviews with the people in various social strata, such as "The Philosophy of Geisha Girls," "The Philosophy of Movie Workers," and so on, as well as a study of individual beliefs of elite members—the equivalent of "This I Believe" in the United States, (b) a series of communication studies especially concentrated on mass culture problems which traditionally academic persons had not tried to explore.

In the studies in communication, the emphasis was put largely on content analysis, for the study of communication for IST was primarily a part of the study of Japanese culture or national character. Their tentative studies of popular fiction and movies, which were published in 1947 as round-table discussions, developed to include field research and produced a book entitled *Yume to Omokage* (Dream and Illusion—Studies on Popular Culture) published in 1950.** The study of popular songs contained in this volume is one of the articles included in that book.

---

* R. P. Dore, "The Tokyo Institute for the Science of Thought—A Survey Report," *The Far Eastern Quarterly,* Vol. XIII, No. 1, November 1953.

** For the publications of IST, see Mr. Dore's article.

As these studies developed, Dr. Hiroshi Minami, a social psychologist, organized another independent organization called the Institute of Social Psychology. Dr. Minami wrote the first standard textbook of social psychology in Japan (1949), and the textbook paid considerable attention to problems of public opinion and mass communication. Consequently, the major subject of The Institute of Social Psychology (hereafter abbreviated as ISP) has been the study of mass media. ISP is one of the few organizations undertaking over-all mass communication studies including audience and effect research.

The IST has published the *Encyclopedia of the Science of Man* (1951) in which problems of communication are well discussed in an interdisciplinary fashion. The items which appeared in the section entitled "Communication" were as follows: communication, mass communication, sign, signify, symbol, language, character, linguistics, Ferdinand de Saussure, Charles Bally, Antoine Meillet, Albert Sechehaye, Otto Jespersen, Edward Sapir, Leonard Bloomfield, Karl Buhler, Nikolai Yacovlevich Marr, comparative linguistics, linguistic sociology, linguistic geography, quantitative semantics, grammar, phonetics, phonology, stylistics, semantics, inner speech form, general semantics, Alfred Korzibsky, mode of signifying, use of signs, type of discourse, history of communication, twilight zone, opposition, argot, basic international language, Lazaro Ludviko Zamenhof, isotype. (Each of these treatments has subunits with cross references to other sections such as "culture," "society," "personality," "logic," etc.)

As to semantics, Mr. Tadatoshi Okubo, a member of IST, organized another group called The Japanese Association for the Study of Language. He, as well as Mr. Tsurumi, has been an introducer of general semantics and he has translated *Language in Thought and Action* by Hayakawa.

Partly stimulated by the efforts of IST and ISP, deep interest in communication was aroused among persons outside of these two organizations. A bibliography entitled "Study of Popular Culture" published by the Japanese Diet Library in 1950 says in its preface, "...Such a task (the analysis of popular culture) has now become the task of outsiders such as sociologists and social psychologists instead of that of specialized literary critics."

On the governmental level, a National Language Research Institute was established and among its publications are such studies as "Newspaper Vocabulary" (1952) and "Women's Magazine Vocabulary" (1953).

In universities, The Newspaper Study Institute of Tokyo University, headed by Professor Yujiro Chiba, has been undertaking both teaching and field research on mass communication. In 1953, a *Readership Survey of Newspapers* was made. Professor Rokuro Hitaka, in The Newspaper Study Institute, at the same time a member of IST, wrote a textbook of sociology with Professor Tadashi Fukutake, in which they emphasized the role of mass communication.

The following were the graduate lecture sujects at The Newspaper Study Institute in 1953:

Research and analysis
    of mass communication .... Prof. Chiba
History of newspapers
    in the Third Republic .... Prof. Kido
Basic theory of mass communication .... Prof. Hitaka

In Kyoto University, at the Institute of Humanistic Science, an informal group for the study of popular culture was organized under Professor Takeo Kuwabara, though most of the people in this group are also members of IST. The characteristic of this group is their well-integrated interdisciplinary effort. The group is rather small, but includes specialists in literature (Prof. Kuwabara, Mr. Tada), history (Mr. Higuchi), psychology (Mr. Fujioka), philosophy (Mr. Tsurumi), and ecology (Mr. Umezao). Their study has been concentrated on an over-all analysis of "Miyamoto Musashi," one of the most popular fictional figures. "The Content Analysis of Miyamoto Musashi" in this volume is one of two articles written on this subject. This group also is holding irregular meetings on popular movies.

Another contribution was made by the members of the Department of Sociology at Gakushuin University, who translated *Mass Communication* by Wilbur Schramm. The translation was directed by Professor Ikutaro Shimizu. Professor Shimizu is one of the leading sociologists in Japan and he wrote a book entitled *Social Psychology* (1953) of which the larger part was occupied by a discussion of mass communication.

Many other universities have courses on communication and journalism, but with little interesting research.

In the commercial sphere, mass communication media such as radio stations, movie producers, and advertising agents, have adopted communications research as a part of their market research. For instance, the Institute of Broadcasting Culture of N.H.K. (the semigovernmental radio station) made an experimental survey by program analyzer in cooperation with The Newspaper Study Institute. Radio Tokyo, a commercial station, has been undertaking a series of audience and effect analyses, and many other radio stations have research departments.

Movie producers have made audience and effect studies in cooperation with ISP, and in fact ISP has been financially supported by this kind of cooperation. The "Haiyu-za" dramatic group is also buying materials concerning its own audience from ISP.

The "Dempo Tsushinsha," the largest advertising agency,

has prepared information as regards readership, coverage, and effects of various media, for its customers (advertisers).

However, most important is the fact that nonprofessional people became interested in the role and importance of mass communication in their communities. Mr. Tsutomu Ono's article in this volume is an example. While most of the studies in mass communication were made by professional people, Mr. Ono's work is an example of a study made by a common man, a factory laborer. He sensed for himself the power of radio in his daily life, in his own community, and he tried to explore the problem by his own devices. From a technical point of view, his study is rough, simple, and even unscientific as far as sampling, interpretation, questionnaire form and so on are concerned. But, his initiative and creativeness in problem formulation are valuable regardless of scholastic mechanics.

Other than Mr. Ono, of course, many workers and young peasants are interested in mass communication problems in their communities, and several articles by such authors have already been published in *"Shiso no Kagaku,"* the organ of IST.

The articles in this volume were all written by the members of the IST, so they may not represent the full range of communication research in Japan. However they are seminal in the sense that all the authors were trying to approach the problems of popular culture which academic people had not previously tried to explore. Besides the articles compiled here, many interesting studies have been published by the members of IST, though some of them are hardly understandable to those who are unfamiliar with Japanese culture itself.

We would like to discuss next some characteristics of communication studies in Japan which may clarify the context in which these articles are written.

III. CHARACTERISTICS OF COMMUNICATION RESEARCH IN JAPAN

As noted before, communication research in Japan emerged in the postwar period under the influence of American social science. However, Japanese scholars developed the research in their own unique directions.

1) *Qualitative rather than Quantitative:*

First of all, we must mention the fact that the studies in this volume were done under very difficult financial conditions hardly believable to American specialists. At best about $100 in American currency is available for the financing of a project. Contributions of free labor by students, or even contributions of their own pocket money, made it possible to undertake field research. Moreover, in the process of sorting and tabulating, no IBM machine or even a simple calculator is available. Consequently, except for a few organizations connected with commercial enterprises, it is impossible for them to conduct large-scale communication research in the American way. This financial stringency is one reason why communication studies in Japan, including the articles in this volume, tend to be qualitative.

However, even if ample funds become available to them, I doubt that Japanese scholars will switch completely to quantitative studies. They are aware of the fact that in such a country as Japan, where the social structure is more complicated than in the United States, techniques used in America will not always reveal the facts of Japanese society. To obtain material on hidden emotions of the people, for example, intensive and qualitative study is a better technique. In other words, they are aware of cultural determinants in the sciences.

2) Culture-Consciousness:

Another important characteristic of communication research in Japan is, as the readers may notice from the articles in this volume, that most of the investigators are using communication research to ascertain characteristics of Japanese culture. In other words, they are studying communication problems as a part of the study of national character. Especially in content analyses of communication, the content is treated as a reflection of the culture.* Mr. Imamura's two articles in this volume, studies in comics and movies, are examples of this tendency.

More important is the fact that in the study of culture, students are not satisfied with mere descriptions of facts. For them, Japanese culture is not only to be studied but also to be reformed. The society itself still contains many feudalistic elements, and the people are living under a traditional value system. The study of culture, including communication research, means much more than study, and it is felt almost a duty for students to make practical applications of their findings. The culture-consciousness of the communication research can be understood in connection with the practical implications of the studies.

3) Reform Movement:

The practical interests of the students of communication vary according to the problems they are dealing with though in principle they are eager to produce a better communication climate in Japan.

However, we can classify the practical implications of communication studies into several categories.

a) The problem of tradition: Contemporary Japanese culture has, as noted by many experts, two major aspects, i.e., traditional and modern. Most of the intellectuals have been so westernized that they tend to disregard the im-

---

* See Mr. Dore's article.

portance of traditional values which exist among the people. Of course, some of the traditional values should be overcome, but before that, it is the common belief of the students that they must face up to the tradition. Precise observation of the tradition is the only basis on which a reform should take place. Mr. Tada's article is an example of this tendency. In almost all of the articles, explicit and implicit discussion of the traditional values appears.

b) *The problem of plurality of communication systems:* The IST has devoted a major effort to breaking the walls which compartmentalized communication in society. In 1946, IST had a project to make technical terms easier, which, in spite of attack from academic people, had great success. In order to establish communication between intellectuals and the common man, the *Shiso no Kagaku,* the organ of the IST, opened its door to everyone who was interested in the study of culture. Mr. Ono's work appeared as the result of this effort. The interdisciplinary principle of IST, which produced *The Encyclopedia of the Science of Man,* succeeded in breaking the fence of specialization among scientists.

c) *The problems of "magic":* Exposing the magic in contemporary mass communication involves political criticism of the governmental authorities. Students criticize politics through the study of communication either explicitly or implicitly. Dr. Minami's article on movies contains a strong protest against the political power behind the commercialism of the mass media. In the process of modernization or democratization of a society, it is almost inevitable for scientists to be more or less political, especially when the government is conservative.

d) *Problems of ambiguity:* The ambiguity of Japanese communication has been explored by Mr. Tsurumi, who collected ambiguous expressions from the daily conversation of peasants. Mr. Okubo, in his various writings, suggested practical techniques to create clearer communication in daily life.

e) Problems of "closed communication": Miss Tsurumi, the elder sister of Mr. Tsurumi, made tremendous efforts to establish interpersonal communication among people who used to live in intrapersonal communication. For instance, she found that in big textile factories, the girls working in the same place scarcely talked to each other except for such everyday phrases as "good morning" or "good-bye." When they are alone, they talk to themselves, inside themselves. Miss Tsurumi felt that to promote good human relationships and friendships among them a more intimate communication system should be created.

She devised a method, based on the experiences of school teachers, by which people belonging to the same social group break their "shells." The method is called "life composition." In a life composition each of the persons writes things which he has experienced, especially things from which he suffered or with which he was dissatisfied. His compositions are read in the group so that the listeners (or readers) can advise or can criticize the writer's way of thinking and behaving. With this approach many people can talk to each other more freely than ever before.

The "Life Counseling" study in this colume started from the same problem. Life counselling is one of the points where intrapersonal communication becomes interpersonal.

IV. PROSPECTS OF COMMUNICATION RESEARCH IN JAPAN

Despite difficulties, students have been eagerly working in the field of communication research. Awareness of the importance of the research is increasing not only among professionals but also among the people at large. We cannot be satisfied with the present level of research, especially as regards mechanical equipment and research techniques. However, with students eager to learn and improve the social and cultural environment in which they are living, the future of communication study in Japan is hopeful and promising.

A BRIEF CHRONOLOGY OF MODERN JAPANESE COMMUNICATION

1846—An abridged translation of the *Netherlands Magazine* for 1839 was published.

1862-5—Several government (Tokugawa)-sponsored newspapers, mainly of international information, were published.

1868—Meiji Restoration.

1869—Newspaper publication was authorized.

1870—First daily newspaper appeared in Yokohama.

1871—Postal regulations completed. Postal service was available between Tokyo and Osaka.

1871-80—Works of J. S. Mill, Rousseau, Shakespeare, Defoe, Dumas, and other basic Western classics were translated and published.

1872—Locomotive introduced.

1873—Telegraph introduced.

1873-4—Major newspapers were founded.

1874—Western techniques of paper manufacturing were sucessfully adopted. First periodical magazine on general topics was published.

1881—First orchestral concert by the Japanese.

1890—Practical use of the telephone.

1896—Cinematograph, Vitascope and other primitive forms of moving pictures were shown to the public in Tokyo.

1900—First professional cartoon appeared in a newspaper.

1903—First movie theater was established in Tokyo.

1907—First illuminated outdoor advertisement.

1909—Phonograph records were manufactured.

1913—Nikkatsu, the first movie company, was established.

1924—Two big newspapers (the Asahi and the Mainichi) each had a circulation of one million copies. First radio broadcasting started by N.H.K., a semi-governmental agency.

1932—First talking picture was produced.

1945—The end of World War II.

1950—First commercial broadcasting station was authorized. The end of N.H.K. network monopoly.

1953—Commercial television was authorized.

THE IMAGE OF AMERICA IN CONTEMPORARY JAPANESE FICTION

by Kenichi Adachi

I. AMERICAN INFLUENCE ON POPULAR TASTE

Such catch phrases as "Kiss-proof lipstick—Now popular in America" are found frequently in advertisements in Japanese newspapers and magazines. The following table indicates the frequency of advertisements thus using American prestige as an appeal in the newspaper Asahi.*

Ads Using American Prestige Appeal

	No. of ads.	No. of pages in paper	Ratio: one ad in every—pages
Dec. 1947	2	70	35
Dec. 1948	2	70	35
Dec. 1949	3	76	25
Dec. 1950	5	96	19
Dec. 1951	10	196	20
Dec. 1952	13	364	28
Dec. 1953	16	376	24
Dec. 1954	12	398	33
Dec. 1955	23	434	19

* The number of pages differs from year to year because of the serious paper shortage during the last ten years.

The advertisers who employ American prestige symbols most frequently are cosmetic and drug companies. Some examples of these catch phrases are:

1) This wonderful Desmos, made in America. (Desmos, rat killer)
2) The raw material is being imported directly from America. (Kiss-me lipstick)
3) In America, people use this daily. (Mix-Bon, vitamin tablet)
4) Our original camera; America wanted to buy our technique! (Arco camera)

One rather new form of American prestige appeal is to say that something "is exported *even* to the U.S."

Another index of Americanism in Japanese popular taste can be found in the names of stores and shops, especially night clubs, cabarets, bars, coffee shops and other entertainment establishments. The following table indicates the distribution of names of these institutions in the city of Osaka, classified by language.*

	Japanese names	English names	Others	Total
Cabarets, night clubs	53	28	16	97
Bars and taverns	110	64	59	233
Coffee shops	275	124	87	486
Total	438	216	162	816

Approximately 26% of Japanese establishments of this sort have English names. For example: Metro, Hollywood, Capital, Queen, Chicago (cabarets); American, Eden, Cadillac, Green, Columbia, Smart, Swan (coffee shops).

We have described only briefly two of the several indications of a growing interest in Americanism as it is reflected in Japanese popular taste. Now we shall try to point out in somewhat greater detail some of the images of

---

* Samples were taken from the yellow pages of the Osaka telephone directory. Osaka is the second largest city in Japan, with a population of roughly 2,500,000.

Americans and of American culture found in present-day Japanese popular fiction. We have chosen for this purpose three examples of popular fiction published within the last two or three years.

II. IMAGES OF AMERICA IN JAPANESE POPULAR FICTION

Popular fiction plays a significant role in Japanese popular culture. Almost without exception, the leading popular fiction is first published in daily newspapers or in other periodicals. It is then usually adapted for the movies, the radio and the stage. Sometimes, a popular song may be written on the basis of the plot. By this chain reaction, a popular story often reaches into the whole structure of popular culture.

In order to describe the image of America found in Japanese popular literature, we have selected three pieces of fiction in which Americans play important roles.

Author	Title	Date of Publication	Medium	Chain Reaction
1. Bunroku Shishi	*Yassa Mossa*	1952	The Mainichi (evening paper)	Book Movie
2. Fusao Hayashi	*Love Affair of My Son*	1954	The Asahi (morning paper)	Book Movie
3. Ayuro Miki	*Bride Wanted*	1955	The Myojo (popular monthly)	Radio Drama Movie

1) Yassa Mossa

The main theme of *Yassa Mossa* is the problem of the illegitimate children of Japanese girls and G.I.'s. The heroine is a housewife who manages an orphanage for these children. Her husband has become a lost soul because of recent social upheavals in Japan, and is of no help to her. Three foreigners appear in this satirical story, an American Negro G.I., a white American lieutenant, and a Canadian businessman.

49

a) Negro G.I.

The Negro G.I. is in love with a prostitute by the name of Bazuka Otoki. The girl, the daughter of a fisherman, has a big neck, dark skin, and very little beauty. She is violent, ignorant, and does not have any affection for the G.I., viewing him purely as a customer. When she is delivered of a mixed-blood child, she places it in the heroine's orphanage. The G.I. believes that the child is his, and continues to send money to his "wife and child," even after his outfit is sent to Korea. He is wounded in the Korean war, and dies leaving a paper which recognizes the child as his own.

The G.I. is described as an extremely good-natured person. When Otoki insists to him that she does not know who is the father of the child, he says, "I love you—this is the evidence." The girl describes him as "a slow, stupidly good guy; he doesn't say 'No' to anything I say. He believes everything I say." The mother of the heroine, an old woman, comments about him: "In this big world, a man like Buddha is living. Don't you think it is interesting that *He* is a colored G.I.?"

However, the G.I. is a rather comical figure, and his "goodness" seems almost synonymous with stupidity.

b) American lieutenant

The lieutenant studied the Japanese language for two years as a language officer and still studies Japanese at the G.H.Q. language school. He is intelligent and interested in the study of Japanese classics and folk arts. In short, he is one of the Americans who know Japan. He is a frequent visitor at the heroine's salon where he talks with other Japanese guests. But no one can judge whether "he is talking seriously or talking jokes." On the surface he is always joking, but essentially he is serious.

The lieutenant's true nature is illustrated by the following episode. He introduces a Canadian businessman to the heroine without knowing that this man is a Don Juan of questionable integrity. When the Canadian tries to approach the heroine, the lieutenant promptly ejects him from the scene. He says to the husband of the heroine, "I did not enjoy doing this. But I could not remain quiet when your family's honor was at stake." He apologizes for his mistake in introducing the Canadian so thoughtlessly. The lieutenant is essentially an individualist who does not interfere in other people's business, but at the same time he feels certain responsibilities.

The lieutenant is regarded as a "pragmatist." As to the heroine's orphanage, he says, "I am not intentionally indifferent to that enterprise, it is merely because I have a principle of avoiding that kind of difficult problem. I have many other things to do." To his words, the heroine says smiling, "Oh, your *pragmatism* again."

The lieutenant is also very practical. He discusses the problem of the illegitimate children with a snobbish Japanese critic. And, "while the critic talks of the desirability of culturally mixed blood, World Government, absolute pacifism, and other abstract topics, the lieutenant wants to discuss things on a more concrete level." He respects traditional Japanese values. When the critic says, "Japanese traditional culture is meaningless," the lieutenant replies, "Do you think so? That sounds very advanced. But don't you feel any contradiction between your negation of Japanese culture and your respect for traditional European values?"

In a word, the lieutenant is described as a representative American gentleman who is practical, sociable, frank, and full of irony and wit. There is a distinct casualness in his behavior.

c) Canadian businessman

The Canadian is a buyer who came to Japan for the negotiation of import and export business. He is really a bad man. With sweet words, he gets involved with several married Japanese women. And as we have seen, he finally approaches the heroine. He also swindles money from Japanese businessmen. He is described by the heroine as "of British origin, having a sort of Mediterranean flavor. His voice, facial expression, and outlook are so tender, naive, and feminine that you cannot imagine that he is Anglo-Saxon." This bad man, as represented by a Canadian, suggests the negative aspects of Americans. He is the embodiment of elements of American immorality during the occupation period. The author mentions such examples as, "a G.I. who went back to his country in spite of his engagement to a Japanese girl," or, "Generally, G.I.'s who are the fathers of these children rarely visit the orphanage. Most of them answer 'No' when they receive letters asking if they recognized their children."

2) Love Affair of My Son

The author, Mr. Hayashi, is a typical "conversional" writer who had been a leftist before the war, was a "Japanist" during the war, and is now a pro-American liberal. His son is studying in the U.S.

This novel is a caricature of the post-war metropolitan atmosphere in which a young man, whose father owns a men's wear store in Tokyo, is perplexed when he is proposed to by several young women at a time. He finally marries a poor but intelligent girl, but in the course of the story, the author describes three women who possess what he calls "Americanistic" qualities. These women are: a Nisei girl from Hawaii, an Americanized Japanese girl, and a Japanese girl who came back from the U.S. after obtaining an M.D. degree there.

a) Nisei girl

Ostensibly, the Nisei girl from Hawaii is the secretary to the president of an import-export company which has an English name. In fact, however, the president is a Chinese from Hong Kong who is engaged in illicit import business, and she is his common-law wife. She is efficient in both the legal and illegal aspects of her husband's business. She is described as beautiful and "about 33 or 34 years of age. She qualifies as a woman president." She becomes acquainted with the hero through her business and soon she says to him, "You are a nice boy. I like you very much. I'll help you make a profit." She is attracted by the hero, but she doesn't crave him. When her invitation for lunch was not accepted she is frank, saying, "Are you afraid of me? Ha, ha, ha—you little fool." Later, her husband marries another woman, and at the same time is accused of illegal activity by the police. Thus the company is closed, and she decides to go back to Hawaii. Her attitude then is commercial and frank. "He (the husband) is a miser. He is a very bad man. He doesn't pay me money. I will take everything in the warehouse and make money. Oh, busy busy! Goddamn! Men are all animals. Ha, ha, ha—." She also says, "He loves another girl. I don't care. But he doesn't pay me consolation money. He is no businessman." In a word, she interprets everything in terms of money, in a purely commercial sense.

Japanese attitudes toward this woman vary. The father of the hero talks of her as "a terrible woman," while the hero himself describes her as "not so terrible because she is always businesslike." He further says, "a woman who is really terrible is one who talks nonsense, like my mother." The materialistic attitude of the Nisei girl is thus approved of by the younger generation, while disapproved of by the older people.

b) Ame-Tara princess

The nickname Ame-Tara princess indicates that this "princess" is a girl who has been interested in Americans, one after another. She is the daughter of an influential businessman, and is very fond of everything American. Her dresses are always bright, "and she likes to let a man carry her baggage, light her cigarette, pay her bills, and do everything for her. She thinks this is a naturally given feminine privilege." This, of course, is an exaggeration of negative aspects of American womanhood. Generally, Japanese men are unfavorable toward the respect which is accorded to women in American culture.

This princess doesn't show the slightest interest in Japanese men. But she thinks any American is "O.K." as long as he is an American. She says: "This time I was proposed to by two Americans. Both are lieutenants. One is a truck driven in Chicago, but he wants at least $100,000 as the dowry. The other has married twice already, but he said that the second divorce is not authorized yet. I don't care about that, although my father is a little afraid of it...Before this, there was a procurator for a Tokyo court for war criminals. He found himself a baroness, and has already gone back to America...Then there was a sergeant. He was childish, cute, kind, and healthy. He was not interested in my dowry at all. His blood was pure. It was so pure that father didn't approve our marriage— he was a pure Negro." However, in spite of her eagerness, all the Americans whom the princess approached go back to their home country.

Most of the Americans whom the princess encounters are either love-hunters or looking for fortune in terms of marriage money. It is significant, as in *Yassa Mossa*, that only the Negro American is favorably described, though he is a rather comical figure.

c) Doctor educated in U.S.

Before going to the United States, the doctor was merely a cute girl, but while she was in America she underwent a surgical operation to make herself perfectly beautiful. Her

54

nose is exactly like Elizabeth Taylor's, her lips like Jean Arthur's, and her figure like Marilyn Monroe's. She is the synthesis of all possible Hollywood beauties. Her voice is musical, but her personality is as "cold as marble." Later she confesses to the hero: "Everybody says that I am pretty, but nobody loves me. A man cannot love a mask."

She could attain perfect beauty by advanced surgical techniques, but what she really obtained was merely an appearance. The author seems to suggest that the progress of technology and science does not solve the problem of the happiness of human beings.

3) Bride Wanted

"Bride Wanted" was published in the "Myojo," a popular magazine with a circulation of over half a million copies. At the same time, the story was broadcast over thirteen local stations as a serial radio drama. The author is a writer for radio and a producer. This story is that of an Issei father who came back to Japan to find a bride after thirty years in the United States. He was accompanied by his Nisei daughter. It is a humorous satire.

a) Issei father

He was born in Kyushu (a southern island of Japan), and went to the United States full of ambition. He succeeded in farming in Minnesota, but he never forgot his home country. Meanwhile, his wife died, leaving him with an only daughter. Now the daughter has finished her college course, and he decides to look for a bride for himself. He wants to marry "a beautiful Japanese woman who was brought up in beautiful Japan." However, the Japan he knows is that of thirty years ago, and he is misinformed about contemporary Japanese social life. He does not even know that there are subways in the larger cities. He brings rice from Minnesota to Japan, because he doesn't know that the serious food shortage is over. The author makes the farmer's outdated knowledge about Japan symbolic of the knowledge possessed by the majority of the American people about present-day Japan.

He believes that "for Japanese women, the traditional kimono costume is most becoming." But in contrast, his own behavior pattern is aggressive and bold.

As soon as he arrives in Japan, he sees a woman on the street in a very sophisticated kimono. He asks her, "Excuse me, are you married?" When she answers, "Yes" with anger, he further asks, "well, then, are you really in love with your husband? Aren't you thinking about divorce?" He is serious in his questioning. The author explains this aggressiveness; "He cannot be concerned with shame or etiquette, because he must find a bride during his very short stay in Japan. There is nothing wrong with a man loving a woman." The author defines this behavior structure as the "frontier spirit." Later the hero tries to get a wife through a T.V. commercial, "Bride Wanted." In this episode, the values of efficiency, love, and adventure which are essentially American are caricatured.

b) *Nisei daughter*

This is the Nisei daughter's first visit to Japan. Her Japanese is very poor. Since she studied social sciences in an American college, she is interested in studying Japanese society and culture. A young T.V. producer is her only relative in Tokyo. She selects him as her interviewee, and asks many questions, even when he is busy in his work. Using the most advanced statistical techniques from America, she asks his income, the number of rooms he has, hours of sleep, kinds of leisure activity, and other questions, all with great intensity. He is sometimes perplexed because occasionally she asks him questions which only Dr. Kinsey should ask. She even goes into the bedroom of this young man to continue her questions. She is a caricature of American positivism.

During her interview, she must have been surprised to learn that her relative doesn't own a car or a T.V. The difference between concepts of wealth in the Japanese and American cultures is one of the elements of humor in this story.

The Nisei daughter has a theory about the happiness of her father. She says to him, "You have sacrificed your happiness in order to bring me up. Now I can be independent, and you have the right to find your own happiness."

Like her father, she is practical. When the T.V. producer hesitates to initiate a plan because of financial difficulty, she tells him, "If you give it up now because you cannot do it you can never do it. Try it. If it fails, think what is wrong with it. And try again. Unless you run your business, the business will run you, you know." When her father hesitates to propose to a woman, she says to him, "Any woman will say 'yes' if you try with passion. Even if she says 'no', try it again and again." Her practical orientation has a certain resemblance to that of the Nisei girl who appeared in the *Love Affair of My Son*.

The author regards the behavior of the father and the daughter as "an expression of the American temperament which is to be friendly with anybody and afraid of nothing."

The only thing which surprises them is the Japanese tradition. Once the father finds an ideal woman and visits her, but he is scared when he hears that she is a viscountess. Also, when the daughter hears from the lady's son, who is a graduate of Oxford, that his family has a history of over one thousand years, she sighs and thinks, "Ten centuries. Not five hundred years have passed since Columbus found America. This boy looks no different from others, but he seemed more respectable once I knew that he was born after one thousand years." The author comments,

"In this respect, the guests from Democracy can say nothing. It may be natural though that they are so awed, because the Americans in general are the only people who admire anything historical." This attitude toward tradition is similar to that of the lieutenant in *Yassa Mossa*. The reason why authors like to present this kind of episode is that historical tradition is one aspect in which they feel Japanese culture is superior to American culture.

III. SUMMARY AND CONCLUSION

Following is a list of items which make up the image of Americans as found in the three pieces of Japanese popular fiction which we have examined.

1) *Positive Items*

Individual trait	Cultural trait
Good-natured	Advanced scientific techniques
Individualistic	Wealthy
Pragmatic	Respect for women
Practical	Knowledge of Japan
Sociable	
Frank	
Responsible	
Childish	
Healthy	
Adventurous	
Efficient	
Aggressive	
Business-like	
Common sense	

2) *Negative Items*

Ignorant	Lack of tradition
Always joking	Respect for women
Careless	Ignorance about Japan
Dishonest	
Commercialism	
Rude	
Sensual	
Superficial sweetness	

In general, as far as the contents of popular fiction are concerned, the image of American culture and Americans is a favorable one. However, two negative aspects are emphasized by these authors: first, that Americans are sensual, and secondly that Americans are fond of material wealth.

Another characteristic is that Negroes are always described favorably. There are two possible reasons for this. First, both Negroes and Japanese feel suppressed by white peoples. Second, such an inferiority complex on the part of the Japanese can be compensated for by looking upon Negroes with a feeling of pity.

A CONTENT ANALYSIS OF LIFE COUNSELING COLUMNS

by Hidetoshi Kato

A "Life Counseling" (Minoue Sodan) column is found in many Japanese newspapers and women's magazines. Readers send letters about their personal troubles, asking professional consultants for solutions.

From a sociological or social psychological point of view, life counseling in the mass media is an interesting and important clue to interpreting contemporary Japanese society and culture.

In recent years, many techniques have been devised to measure attitudes. We respect these efforts and hope for their progress. But sometimes questionnaire-and-answer type research has a weakness in that the answers are not spontaneous. People are forced to answer questions on which they are not well informed.

While the readers who write letters for life counseling are not a valid cross-section of the Japanese people, yet theirs are voluntary opinions on various problems in some detail.

Life counseling letters are not like letters to the editor.

Letters to the editor contain more or less definite conclusions about something. Life counseling letters do not express any conclusion. They describe people's situations and ask authorities for a solution. Hence it may be possible, through the analysis of life counseling letters, to ascertain the problems with which people are confronted.*

I. INTRODUCTION AND THE SAMPLE USED

"When you have any difficult personal problem, do you generally consult either family or friends?" To this question 84% of a Japanese adult population sample answered "Yes" and over 40% of those who answered "Yes" further replied that they do "as suggested by the consultant."** Counsel is clearly an important factor in determining an individual's behavior orientation. Through various kinds of counseling, people are relieved from feelings of loneliness and instability, and by having answers from consultants they try to make the basis of their behavior more objective. The "life counseling" described in our present

---

* Like other popular communications, such as popular songs, fiction, radio and TV programs, the importance of life counseling was completely neglected by scholars. This study of it was originally proposed in Japan by Professor Shunsuke Tsurumi, and several members of the Institute of Science of Thought have engaged in an inter-disciplinary survey of this subject. This paper is a translation of one of the reports which appeared in *Me* magazine, (organ of the Institute), No. 8-9, 1953. For reference we list here the full table of contents of the original edition:

Akio Saki :	The Origin of Life Counseling.
Hajime Ikeuchi :	A Historical Survey of Life Counseling in Newspapers.
Motoichi Nogami :	Life Counseling in Postwar Europe (fortune-tellers).
Hidetoshi Kato :	A Content Analysis of Life Counseling.
Kazuko Tsurumi :	Logical Examination of Life Counseling as Related to Communication and Discommunication Problems.
Eiko Ohama :	As a Consultant.
Nobue Sato :	The Philosophy of Life Guidance (an essay).

** "Public Opinion Series: On Social Education," National Bureau of Public Research, March 1953, p. 25.

study, is, however, merely one type of counseling. It may be distinguished from other forms by three criteria:

(1) It is done for readers of a mass medium. The problem and its solution are published as human interest material.

(2) The consultants are not such ordinary consultants as family or friends but professional experts or authorities.

(3) Unlike legal counseling, life counseling deals with moral problems.

Surveying mass media which contain life counseling we found the following.

(1) Newspapers: 24 daily newspapers (including one nationally circulated paper the *Yomiuri*) have life counseling columns.

(2) Magazines: Almost every women's magazine. Popular magazines such as *Heibon, Myojo,* etc., have a few pages devoted to counseling.

(3) Radio: The only case is a life guidance program on Radio Tokyo.

In this article, the *Yomiuri* newspaper and the *Heibon* magazines were used for the sample. The *Yomiuri* is the only paper among the "big three" Japanese newspapers which has a life counseling column, and, as Professor Ikeuchi has pointed out, it was the *Yomiuri* which developed life counseling in the mass media. *Heibon* is a post-war magazine with an extraodinary circulation (over 1,000,000) among the younger gentration. Its contents are mostly movie stories and fiction.

The number of letters which those two media receive and their backgrounds are as follows:

(1) *Yomiuri:* Around 50 letters are received every day. The writers are about equally divided between the sexes though male clients are concentrated around the age of 25 or younger while females are generally over 30. The women's section of the *Yomiuri* handles the column.

(2) *Heibon:* The number of letters is about 50 daily. The majority of the writers are high school girls of the ages 16-19. As we shall see, the contents of their letters center around the body.

From these letters, a few are selected and published with "responsible" answers. The selection is made "to serve the common interest of the readers" (editor of the *Yomiuri*) or "to appeal to the young generation" (*Heibon*), so that we cannot infer the general trend of the content from those which are published.

In order to avoid the distortion brought about by editorial selection we borrowed approximately 200 original letters from the editor of *Heibon*. However, since *Yomiuri* has strict regulations to protect the privacy of the writers, we had to be satisfied with those letters published in the paper.

There is no valid basis for assuming that those who send letters for counseling are a representative sample of the Japanese population nor that the letters which we used in our analysis are representative of all life counseling letters. We cannot generalize from this material to the full nature of the problems from which the Japanese people are suffering. This study is an analysis of life counseling as it appeared in a few mass communications.

II. THE CLASSIFICATION OF THE CONTENTS

It is not easy to find a sound basis for classifying the content of the letters, as each problem is unique and delicate. However, we employed the following categories describing dimensions of individual and group relationships.

(a) Problems of the individual's body which may include psychosomatic problems. (Example: "How can I make my ugly legs smart?")

(b)   Problems which occur in one-to-one human relations. (Example: "My boy friend is changing his mind.
How can I get his love again?")

(c)   Problems which occur in group or institutional
situations. (Example: "My parents are against our marriage. Is there any way to persuade them?")

Letters to the two mass communication media were
classified according to this scheme and the comparative
result is indicated in Table I.

Table I   Classification of the Contents

		Yomiuri Letters	Heibon Letters
(A)	Physical	22	143
(B)	One-to-one human relations ...	15	58
(C)	Group human relations	91	21
		128	222

We shall analyze these three types of problems in the
following sections.

III. PHYSICAL PROBLEMS AS SEEN IN HEIBON'S COUNSELING COLUMN

Characteristically the letters received by the editors of
Heibon concentrate on physique; even problems of human
relations are reduced by the readers to physical problems.
These physical problems are, however, not medical since
most of the clients complain of their physical disadvantage
as an obstacle to adjusting in their human relations.

"I am working in bus transportation. But my brothers
laugh at my fat legs, and for the same reason I cannot get
a boy friend." "My breast is very big so I am very ashamed
when I am among my friends." "The mark of a burn
which I got when I was a child still remains on my face.
Because of this mark I failed in love."

The clients who ask counseling on physical problems,
in short, regard their physical handicap or abnormality as
a disadvantage in their social activities.

Table II indicates the distribution of physical handicaps or abnormalities, at least as perceived by the letter writers.

Table II

	Division		Subdivision	Number	Total
1)	Constitution	a)	Constitution in general (fat, short, etc.)	13	
		b)	Nose (small, short, red, etc.)	11	
		c)	Shape of face	6	
		d)	Breasts	6	
		e)	Eyes (squint eyes, etc.)	7	
		f)	Legs (fat, short)	4	
				—	47
2)	Configuration of face	a)	skin (pimples, moles, etc.)	10	
		b)	color (dark)	6	
		c)	hair (frizzled, etc)	9	
		d)	burns or scars	6	
				—	31
3)	Psychosomatic	a)	blush easily	3	
		b)	communication (stammer)	4	
		c)	sweat profusely	4	
				—	16
4)	Sex	a)	sexual organ (male)	28	
		b)	sexual organ (female)	15	
				—	43
5)	Sickness			6	6
			Total		143

Examples:

1-a "I don't like to see people talking about my fat body. Please suggest some diet for me."

1-b "I am a girl 19 years old. I have a boy friend whose nose is very smartly shaped. He may be ashamed of me who has this small nose. And I would like to undertake necessary medical operation. Will you please tell me about reliable doctors?"

1-d "I am 18. My constitution is average except for these extraordinary big breasts. Please tell me how I can make them smaller."

1-f "I had a chance to be acquainted with a young man for 9 months. But because of my fat legs he has left me.

Mine are three times bigger than average. Please solve my trouble."

2-a "I don't like to go to school these days. The reason is the pimples spread over my face."

From these examples it will be clear that most of the inquiries about physique arise from assuming that a non-average physique is a disadvantage in social life.

This kind of fixation on physical conditions contains some neurotic tendencies which we shall examine later. However, this fixation is not only a problem of abnormal psychology but also a problem of Japanese culture. As the social background of concentration on physique, we may mention the following two cultural charateristics.

1) The Expression of Social Status Through Physique:

In Japanese society, any given occupation or social status is apt to be expressed through a man's physical appearance. As Professor Mochizuki has said, "In Japan, when one praises another's physique, he is not talking about his physical condition itself but saying, 'your status is well expressed by your physique.'" What writers to life counsellors desire is a physique suitable to their appropriate social status.

2) The Desire for Unity of Standards:

The formation of physique stereotypes is related to the single valued orientation which can be found in all aspects of Japanese culture. People are accustomed to be obedient to one single value (such as the Emperor's authority), and this obedience has been the security system for the Japanese people. Japanese cannot feel at ease when lacking clear social expectations in various situations. They want unified and ideal types for everything, and physique also is one of the objects which should be standardized.

The desire for unity of standards is not only a Japanese problem. It is found in all highly mechanized modern societies. However, in Japan it is a carry-over from the feudal ages.

In other words, clients of *Heibon's* life counseling suffer from the fact that they do not have average or standard physiques which the culture approves. They are eager to approach the ideal type by improving their bodily structure.

But what are these standards from the clients' point of view? It should be noted here that there exist two different cultural values in contemporary Japanese society. Because of several years of occupation by the United States, the ideals that exist may be designated Ideal-Japanese and Ideal-American. The contents of the letters convey the conflict between the ideals of physique in the two cultures.

Ideal Physique ("A" means American influenced)

Constitution ....tall   "A"
Nose   ....high "A"
Face   ....round shape
Breast ....small and large, a conflict of values
Legs   ....thin and long
Color ....white
Hair   ....black

Special attention should be paid to nose and breast. As to the nose, the Japanese traditional value was said to be well-shaped with medium height. (*Hanasuji ga toru*). So the desire of girls to make their noses high "like Elizabeth Taylor," may be regarded as an example of Americanization.

As to the breasts, the Japanese value has been small-ness. But girls who complain that theirs are "too big" are also well aware of the opposite value. One of them states, "I know that some girls feel it trouble that their breasts are too small and I read that bigger ones are more attractive. But I do not know which is better."

Since most of the advertisements of cosmetics and women's clothes are illustrated by American girls, Japanese girls feel a conflict as to their ideal-type.

IV. EMPHASIS ON PHYSIQUE IN HUMAN RELATIONS PROBLEMS: AN ANALYSIS OF CATEGORY (B)

In *Heibon*, most of the problems which involve troubles in human relations concern one-to-one relations, that is boy-girl problems. Some write presenting their love-getting problems in romantic sentimental ways with dramatization of themselves. Some are full of sentimentality about broken hearts.

However, about 60% of the letters are not of this kind. They tell their stories and troubles, but their troubles are reduced to physical or biological ones. They are sex problems, not moralistic, but biological ones.

Most of the letter writers have lost their loves, but they are not asking for salve for a broken heart. Their problem is virginity.

"When I was quite ignorant about this kind of thing, I happened to have a relation with a boy. I was foolish."

"He took me to a small inn in a small town and promised that he would marry me...I came back home crying."

These girls are nervous about their lost virginity. They seem to have the traditional social norm that virginity is a most important thing for good girls who are going to marry. They are anxious about their mistake, but their concern is not moralistic or ethical nor a feeling of guilt, but biological and practical. They regret that they committed a mistake, but they formulate their problems as follows:

"Is it possible for me to marry another man without telling him my mistakes?"

"I wonder whether a man can recognize me as a non-virgin."

They do not think it is ethically wrong but disadvantageous in terms of future marriage. Some of them are afraid only of the possibility of pregnancy. In a word, the pattern of love affair inquiries is that of girls viewing the problem of virginity biologically, not ethically. This tendency may be viewed as one more example of the *après guerre* generation's philosophy of carnality.*

V. PROBLEMS OF GROUP RELATIONS AS SEEN IN *YOMIURI'S* COUNSELING COLUMN

About 70% of the letters published in *Yomiuri* concern problems which occur in groups or institutions. (See Table I.) In what sort of groups do these troubles take place? Table III shows that most take place in the family.

Table III

Groups in Which Problems Take Place

(1)	Family and kinship group	75
(2)	Friends or school	3
(3)	Occupational group	3
	Total	81

As pointed out by many authors, the human relations within the family are among the dominant and characteristic relations in Japanese society. It will not, therefore, be

---

*The "liberation" of sex was one of the most distinctive features of post-war Japanese society. In the field of literature such authors as Taijiro Tamura, Seiichi Funabashi, Sakunosuke Oda, became best-sellers because of their bold treatment of the problem of sex and its liberation. In addition there was an influence from American culture, especially through movies. The reconsideration of sex is essentially a reaction against rigid feudalistic morals between man and woman. Also at the time of confusion after the war, the revaluation of sex found philosophical support in existentialism. See "A Content Analysis of Tamura's Writing," by Hyosuke Kuro.

surprising that most of these problems center around family relations.

Table IV further indicates who is complaining about whom in the family as related to their status in the family.

Table IV

Classification of Conflicts in the Family Group

Child about parent	21
Parent about child	4
Total parent-children relations	25
About parents-in-law	5
About children-in-law	1
Total parent-children-in-law relations	6
Wife about husband	20
Husband about wife	11
Total husband-wife relations	31
Older sibling about younger sibling	7
Younger silbling about older sibling	5
Total brother-sister relations	12
About relatives	1
Total	75

It is evident from the Table that most of the letter writers are of inferior status in the family. This is most notable in the balance between letters from parents and children. As an expert on the Japanese family system pointed out, "the relations of parents and children were expected by the conservatives to be the last line of compromise after the family system was at least legally abolished." The following are examples of inquiries on this topic:

1) Complaints from Children about Parents:

"The other day on my way from school I felt a headache and dropped in at a friend's house to take a rest. But as soon as I came back home, my father scolded me without listening to my apology: he insisted that I was late for supper."

"These days my father drinks every day, saying that he is invited to a party...but, actually he is having a special relation with a Geisha girl. I saw the other day they went to a restaurant together. I advised him several times, but he always says, 'It's not your business.' "

"Because my family is poor, I could not go to college, but anyway I think I must get a job and be independent. However, since my father has absolute authority about every domestic matter, he wants me to take a job which I do not like. The same thing happened when my elder sister found a job which he did not like. Is it approved for fathers to interfere in the choices of a child?"

2) Complaints from Wife about Husband:

"We spent fourteen years together. But he has never told me the exact amount of his salary. He used to give me some money every month, but I am like a slave who must manage housekeeping with this small amount of money. Whenever I complain about this problem, he beats me."

"Twenty-five year old housewife, married four years ago. He has disappeared for past six months without notice. He might have gone with another girl."

Inquiries concerning family relationships are a natural reflection on the irrational family system.

VI. SOCIAL PSYCHOLOGY OF LIFE COUNSELING

The contents of some of the letters are so dramatic that many people doubt their authenticity. However, the letters which we obtained do not seem spurious, though subjective selections are made by the editors.

Among these letters we find several elements of interest from the point of view of abnormal social psychology. In this section we want to deal briefly with social pathological aspects of life counseling.

First of all, it should be noted that most of the letters which fall into category (A) or letters about physique express a feeling of inferiority.

As we have noted, these people are nervous because some of their physical qualities are not ideal or standard. They, therefore, think of themselves as inferior persons. As a result they hesitate to write their names and addresses correctly. Most of the letters lack a return address.

Since these writers are nameless, isolated, and inferior (at least in their own view) they internalize their trouble and regard themselves as the most powerless creatures in society. This feeling of isolation and helplessness may be well explained in terms of Eric Fromm's concept of social masochism.

(1) Sometimes the masochistic tendency in life counseling clients appears in the form of exhibitionism. Clients describe their physical abnormalities very precisely, especially in the case of sexual organs.

(2) The desire to become average or ideal can itself be seen as an expression of social masochism. The clients want to identify themselves with socially-approved ideals disregarding their actual and given attributes. They are not sure enough of themselves to develop their own way independently and individually.

(3) A masochistic tendency may also be seen in the relationship between clients and the "authorities" they consult. Since the consultants employed by newspapers are viewed as experts in their respective field, the fact of receiving advice means more to the clients than the advice *per se*. Actually clients await not the consultant's *advice* but his *orders*. They cannot judge their own situations

for themselves, so they want to find authorities who can judge. According to Fromm this complete reliance on experts is a symptom of social masochism. The stereotypic concluding sentence in these letters is "I don't know what I should do! Please help me."

People are looking for a magic helper from outside. In the extreme case, this tendency appears as neurosis.

"Isn't there any way I can be taller? I am worrying because I may be excluded from society." (The height of this 17 year old girl is 160 cm., which actually is average.)

"I think I had better kill myself, for I, who lost virginity, cannot get married ever."

These are the extreme cases in which the feeling of insecurity became a kind of obsessive compulsive neurosis.

Again, if we may use Fromm's concept, the masochistic tendencies seen in life counseling can be generalized into the concept of "receptive orientation." (See: E. Fromm, *Man For Himself*, 1949, Chapter 3, Section II.) The concept of receptive orientation can also serve as an explanatory principle in the study of many other aspects of Japanese culture.

In Japanese society, there are many hierarchical compartmentalizations of social groups, and the basic human relations are based on a family or pseudo-familistic model. The Emperor has absolute authority over the people, landlords over tenants, parents over children, men over women, and so on. This kind of rule-and-obedience relationship was, and still is, the traditional Japanese social behavior pattern. The Japanese are forced to live "properly" in accordance with various external indices, such as age, sex, occupation, residence, etc. [See such frames of reference as "...*like*" (*rashiku*), "...tempered" (*katagi*).] In a word, individuality is suppressed by social expectations.

The give-it-up logic, which is frequently found in Japa-

nese popular songs, is an expression of the feeling of power-
lessness. And, of course, sometimes frustration is trans-
formed into aggressiveness. Consequently, the Japanese
want to find something on which they can rely. If they
can find such a thing, they feel secure. In this respect,
there is no difference for the Japanese people between
Ideal-Japanese and Ideal-American; both are authorities
approved by society. The former was dominant in the
pre-war period while the latter appeared in post-war
Japan; but the attitude of the people to the two values
was similar.

VII.   CONCLUSION*

We have attempted, in the preceding sections, to analyze
the contents of life counseling columns. Both the technique
and materials of the study are only partially valid, and
it may not be altogether sound to generalize to the problems
of contemporary Japanese culture from this analysis.
However, the analysis seems to give us some suggestions
and hints concerning the function of counseling in society.

When in trouble, people turn to counsel. Counseling is
an important pattern of communication in human life.
The cooperative problem-solving by the client and the
consultant develops their thoughts as well as the society
to which they belong. Life counseling columns lack this
general value of counseling in society. The consultants in
life counseling formulate a problem on an improper level.

Marxists, on the one hand, formulate problems on a
wrong level in the sense that they believe every contemporary problem can be solved in terms of contradictions
in capitalist society, so that such minor problems as

---

* After this article was published, the study of life counseling
was continued by some members of IST, and their study, including
the historical observation of problems, was published in the form
of a book titled, *Life Counseling,* Kawade Shobo Publishing Co., 1956.

erythrophobia of a person may be explained by them as the result of capitalism. They want to widen every personal problem situation to a social problem. On the other hand, in life counseling, every problem is narrowed down to a very personal problem. When, for instance, a trouble in a family is presented by a client, the consultant suggests "be patient" and tells her that "everything will be all right if you try to be nice to every one." Even a social problem such as unemployment is interpreted as a personal problem. They tell the client that the reason why he cannot find a job is because he is not an able man or because he is lacking in eagerness to find a job, and so forth.

Every human problem has its unique character and the level of problem solution depends on the character of the problem. This is the starting point of counseling. But contemporary counseling is completely blind in the sense that it is based on the belief that there is only one level for problem solving.

THE LITERATURE OF THE FLESH: A STUDY OF MR. TAIJIRO TAMURA'S THOUGHT

by Tadatoshi Okubo

Editor's note: Carnality was one of the dominant themes in postwar Japanese culture, though by now this fad has practically disappeared. The article here translated is a condensation of a manuscript of the same title which appeared in the *Science of Thought (Shiso no Kagaku)*, Vol. 4, No. 3, 1949.

One's first reaction to Mr. Tamura's writings is that he knows how to write an interesting story, but one whose interest is of a dangerous kind.

He tells us that he is going to explore the human body. "I found that the strongest if not the only human impetus is the biology of the body. Therefore, I believe in the liberation of the body and in the study of the body."

It is an advance to bring out into the sun topics which used to be suppressed in our public prints. Since "man is an animal that enjoys the pleasure of responding to stimuli he himself sought out," one cannot wholly despise those who follow the literature of the body and other erotica. The range of their readers varies from youth to middle age and even includes older people, though the majority are young men and women.

Mr. Sakaguchi, another writer of the same group, says: "It is natural for youths who become aware of their bodies to be interested in thinking and knowing about them. It is as natural as that they should seek for something about their souls.

In practice, Japanese sex morality is still confined by feudalistic familism. An adult's attitude towards love and marriage remains as it was in his middle-school days. It is no wonder that the sudden change in our society has caused extreme confusion in morals.

However, Mr. Tamura's work is dangerous because it is exclusively concerned with liberation of sexuality (as he understands it). The establishment of a new sex morality he neglects completely. Regarding this point, he has said: "An individual, or a people, sometimes faces a situation in which he must develop, even if it be by destroying the established morality and order. The temporary confusion thus produced is not a problem at all." In a sense, this approach is similar to the kind of revolutionary theory which insists that in order to develop, things should first be destroyed. However, a revolutionist has at least some idea of what kind of things should be established after destruction. Mr. Tamura emphasizes liberation and destruction, but does not offer the slightest suggestion on the nature of the new value system.

I. MR. TAMURA'S VIEWPOINT ON LITERATURE

1) Mr. Tamura is Skeptical about Ideology:

"I wonder if ideas have contributed anything to the betterment of contemporary Japan, full as it is of black-marketing, crime, prostitution, and hunger. The established ideology still preaches its time-worn doctrines to us. We, however, reject all ideology." "All Japanese thinkers and novelists are chronic liars. Their condition is so chronic that they are not aware that they are liars."

2) Mr. Tamura is also Skeptical of Logic and Rationality:

"Because of my seven years of army life, I am like a baby and I cannot think logically." "I do not believe in anybody who talks logically." "The entire old system has lost its prestige. I cannot trust knowledge, rationality, and morality."

3) The Body as a Tool for Grasping Reality:

"If we cannot believe in our heads, the only way to see the ever-changing reality is to feel it and experience it by means of our bodies." "Our distrust of ideas is so total that the only thing we can believe in is our bodies. One's body is the only truth. Pain, desire, anger, ecstacy, agony, and sleep—these are the only things which are true. Only by these do we become aware of our existence." "I think the pursuit of my own body is identical to the pursuit of my thought. I cannot conceive of the existence of thought as independent from body."

4) Mr. Tamura's View of the Prospect for a Revolution of Man in Japan:

"The author's aim is the revolution of man. In the Western world man has been liberated through the Renaissance and the French Revolution. Japan had the Meiji Restoration and other reformations, but they did not result in the liberation of man. It is my firm belief that this is the time for it." "We must be men who are worthy to be men. To be so, we must liberate our bodies freely and let them be as natural as a baby's. In this way, we shall be able to find out what a man is."

5) Mr. Tamura's Ideal Japanese:

"I think we must make the body of the Japanese fat and big. We must then build a firm humanity on the basis of this body. That is the only way in which we can create a man who overcomes Japanese sentimentality and is free of the assumptions of contemporary common sense."

6) Mr. Tamura's Ideal of What Literature Should Be:

"Our literature should be more confused, more destructive, more erotic, and more eccentric, as befits the literature of a defeated nation. These characteristics are the natural result of our defeat in war, and if our literature does not have them, it is a lie and a pretense." He also suggests that eroticism is a kind of safety valve: "Many people, including a scholar at Nagoya Medical University, have pointed out how surprising it is that Japan is now experiencing less confusion than one might have expected. This is because eroticism is not suppressed. Young people have an outlet for their sexual desires in reading erotic publications. That protects them from overt sexual crimes."

By now it should be clear that Mr. Tamura writes with the following purposes in mind:
1. To destroy the established morality.
2. To negate the established ideology and logic.
3. To prove that one's body is the sole reality.
4. To initiate the liberation of man through the body.
5. To describe a new ideal Japanese type.
The following table lists the representative writings of Mr. Tamura (both fiction and essays) and indicates their basic content.

The first finding from this chart is that 24 stories out of 35 contain a more or less graphic description of sexual intercourse. Also, in 13 cases out of 35, the author describes the process by which a virgin is deflowered. Moreover, except in one case, this kind of affair does not result in marriage. These two points are the basic characteristics of Mr. Tamura's works as respects the relationship between hero and heroine.

There is also an interesting distribution of occupations

79

Title	Hero	Heroine	The Relationship	Description of Sexual Intercourse
A. Body is the Man				
B. Preface to "Gates of the Flesh"				
C. Woman and the Flesh	Essays			
D. Opinions of Mr. Tamura				
E. Gates of the Body	criminal	prostitute	prostitution	yes
F. Demons of the Flesh	soldier	Communist maid	V-S	yes
G. The Story of a Prostitute	soldier	prostitute	prostitution	yes
H. The Gates of the College	student	girl student	love-marriage	no
I. The Grudge	rapist	office girl	V-S	yes
J. Blue Apple	illustrator	dancer	kiss	no
K. A Lover	boxer	waitress	cohabitation	yes
L. Middle Age Passion	producer	a madame	escape	no
M. Elegy	ex-soldier	wife of another soldier waiting for her husband	xx	no
N. Girls	policeman	his daughter	prostitution of her friend	no
O. In a Destroyed Town	ex-soldier	waitress	memory	no
P. A Queen is Born	ne'er-do-well	waitress	xx	yes
Q. The Robbers Laugh	ex-soldier	xx	xx	no
R. Friendship	executive	woman reporter	love	no
S. The Story of a Criminal Woman	criminal (ex-soldier)	pickpocket (ex nurse)	V-S	yes
T. Body: Male and Female	blackmarketeer	dancer	V-S	yes
U. Woman Speaks	writer	waitress	xx	yes
V. Woman Hunted	reporter	dancer	xx	yes
W. Kawa Semi	ex-soldier	mistress	xx	yes
X. A Pair of Pickpockets	pickpocket	pickpocket	V-S	yes
Y. Women of the Town	blackmarketeer	waitress	V-S	yes
Z. The Secret of a Beauty	young man	waitress (prostitute)	prostitution	yes
a. Town in the Night	blackmarketeer	waitress	love	no
b. Independent Sisters	lover of the younger sister	dancer	xx	yes

c.	A Cage	soldier	Communist maid	V-S	yes
d.	A Morning Glory	ex-soldier	his sister	xx	yes*
e.	Fog	writer (ex-soldier)	reporter	xx	yes
f.	Around Asahi-cho	writer (ex-soldier)	prostitute	V-S	yes
g.	Anxious Woman	ex-soldier	dancer-prostitute	xx	yes
h.	Like an Animal	dancer	singer	V-S	yes
i.	Thinking of Man	executive	office girl	V-S	yes
j.	A Taken Flower	painter	secretary	xx	yes
k.	Night in Atami	ex-soldier	dancer	V-S	yes
l.	A Man who Loves Stars	blackmailer	prostitute	love	no
m.	Reunion	blackmarketeer	waitress	V-S	yes

V—S   means that a virgin loses her virginity in the story.
* In this particular case, Mr. Tamura describes sexual contact between a brother and his younger sister.

for the hero and heroine in Mr. Tamura's fiction. The following table indicates occupational classifications for significant characters.

Male		Female	
Ex-soldier	13*	Prostitute	12
Blackmarketeer	8	Waitress	9
Gangster	3	Dancer	9
Small blackmarketeer	2	Office girl	3
Ne'er-do-well	2	Reporter	3
Painter	2	Pickpocket	2
Executive	2	Chinese Communist maid	2
Writer	2	Housewife	2
College student	2	College student	2
Blackmailer	1	Madame	1
Pickpocket	1	Secretary	1
Town boss	1	Designer	1
Boxer	1	Actress	1
Musician	1		
Singer	1		
Reporter	1		
Publisher	1		
Editor	1		
Illustrator	1		
Producer	1		
Poet	1		
Soldier	1**		

* Ex-soldier indicates a soldier who became a civilian after the war. They overlap with blackmarketeers, or criminals.
** Soldiers in Mr. Tamura's work appear only twice. They are Japanese soldiers in China, and in both cases they have contact with Communist maids.

II. THE DESTRUCTION OF THE OLD MORALITY

The means by which Mr. Tamura tries to break down the old morality are as follows:
1. The justification of robbery and other crimes;
2. The justification of blackmarketeering;
3. Treating prostitution merely as a business;
4. Negating respect for virginity;
5. Treating sexual activity as a natural thing.

Mr. Tamura's Views of the Law:

"There is no such thing as law or morality in this world. These things were burned out by war." (E) "In the eyes of these girls [prostitutes] who get together in order to make a living, Ibuki [the hero, a burglar] is an attractive type of man, since he is full of drive in the struggle for existence. They look upon him with admiration. There is no difference between them and women in primitive society." (E) "He stole purses and watches especially from blackmarketeers, and the nouveaux riches."

Mr. Tamura Justifies Blackmarketeering:

"It is understandable that since many people lost their jobs they now engage in blackmarketeering." (T) "Because something is wrong with my soul, I can do anything including blackmarketeering. Setsuko [a girl], you, your mother, and your children, all of you are able to live because my soul is distorted." (M) However, the character speaking these lines has no feeling of guilt for his distortion. He is rather proud of himself for being a blackmarketeer.

Mr. Tamura Justifies Prostitution:

"We cannot say that prostitution is wrong simply because it is not permissible under the old morality." (D) "Why am I wrong to do what I wish with my body? Why do you say that I am a criminal?"—"Tell me when and how we [prostitutes] disturb the people." (N) "I even think that in a sense prostitutes live their lives more sincerely than we do." (H)

Mr. Tamura Does Not Respect Virginity:

"No, I am not a virgin now, but does that mean that I have lost my value? Was my only value that I was a virgin? Did you love me only because I was a virgin?" (I)

It is apparent from the table of Mr. Tamura's works that his heroines lose their virginity easily and quickly. It seems intolerable for him to think of respect for a virgin.

III. THE STRUCTURE OF THE OLD MORALITY

Essentially the old morality which Mr. Tamura is challenging is based on feudalistic familism. "The Way of the Subject," a national textbook during the War, said: "A household in our country is an inheritance from our ancestors, and its organization centers around the head of the house. In other words, ours is different from the Western world's in that in the West a family is composed primarily of a husband and wife, while with us it is composed basically of parents and sons." "The husband and wife relationship is less important than the generation relationship. A wife marries not only her husband but also his family. In recent years, misleading Western ideas have been introduced into our country, but it is our pleasure to observe that this trend is disappearing."

The following statements quoted from a woman's magazine of 1930, represent the old feudal morality with regard to love and marriage.

"The soul of a young girl is like a baby in society. You must bear in mind that it is as dangerous to leave her alone as to leave a baby alone. She may be spoiled without her mother's care. It is your duty as a mother to control her free activities such as meeting boys, going to movies. . . . The first and the most important qualification of a bride is virginity. Girls who lose their virginity are not qualified to marry. A girl must defend her virginity to the death. . . . There are some people who say that marriage should start with love and that marriage without love is meaningless, but these are dangerous words. . . . Investigation by a girl's parents is most desirable. You must investigate a man's status, lineage, family, property, occupation, skill, and everything." (*Shufu No Tomo* Magazine, January, 1930.)

As we have noted, Mr. Tamura is thoroughly opposed to that point of view, and says: "Anyway, we must destroy all ideas of love based on feudalistic morality—this is the healthiest way to live in the present—a new morality is a problem for the future." (I)

In attempting to break down the old morality, Mr. Tamura has described in detail the nude human body, both male and female, as well the sexual desire of women, the ecstasy of sexual intercourse, and other erotic subjects. In one extreme case, he even wrote about sexual contact between a man and his younger sister. (d)

IV. MR. TAMURA'S VALUE SYSTEM

As we saw in the preceding sections, Mr. Tamura disregards the existing moral system. In his scheme, it seems to us, he is seeking the basis of a new morality in the norms of an ingroup which is mostly anti-social in character. He is not looking for a morality on which society as a whole can be based. In his famous "Gates of the Body" he wrote about the norms of the prostitute group as follows: "Among them [prostitutes], there is a kind of norm of the herd. For example, if a girl offers her body to a man without proper reward, she must be punished very severely, because such an act is a threat to their business—They have their own territories. If a stranger is found poaching in their territory, she should be punished by lynching." (E) "One of them fell in love with a student, and did not take any payment from him. In punishment for this they cut her hair short like a soldier's and purged her from the group."

1) Mr. Tamura's Sense of Happiness:

"If I were asked why one was born, I would answer that it was to be happy. Everybody is living for his happiness, isn't he? Even the Communists' aim is the happiness of the people. I think that generally happiness means money, because money can do everything. Bu I also think that the most important ingredient in happiness is sexual. The reason the proletarian hates the rich man is, to a certain degree, that the rich man can have any woman in the world at his will." (g)

2) Mr. Tamura Justifies Everything in Terms of the War:

"Even my mother doesn't know that I am living this way (as a prostitute). She really thinks that I earn all this money from my job in the tea-room. All of this is because of the War." (Z) "He began to do something wrong after he came back from the army and found that his family was practically starving." (S) "In this changing world, it is indeed surprising that a woman who lost her lover in the war can continue to live." (X)

However, Mr. Tamura does not analyze the War itself. Instead he attacks critical ideas about the War as ideology without flesh.

V. CONCLUSION

To summarize, let me make a list of the pros and cons of Mr. Tamura's way of thinking.

1) Pros:

1. His works are interesting as entertainment.
2. He bravely attacks the old system of morality.

2) Cons:

1. In his conception, the body means only a bundle of sexual pleasures.
2. He exaggerates sexual pleasure.
3. He makes readers, especially younger ones, think of the opposite sex only in terms of physical sex.
4. He makes readers disregard ideas, philosophy, and other spiritual values.
5. He justifies any and all anti-social activities. He is at odds with criticism of these activities.

6. In his value scale, criminals, prostitutes and black-marketeers are ascribed more prestige than those who work honestly.

7. His works decrease the will to work, and make people think less about their significance in society.

8. He makes no distinction between the liberation of the body and sexual anarchy.

Mr. Tamura and other writers of the carnal school are no longer as popular as they were in 1946. In fact the *Yomiuri* newspaper of July 1948 reported that "That group of erotic magazines has almost disappeared. Even a 10-yen price cannot attract readers."* However, from a social psychological point of view, this type of literature is still worthy of careful study and analysis because the popularity of carnality was a product of a time of social disorganization when people lost faith in the existing system of values. The study may give us a clue to such times.

---

* This should not leave the impression that erotic magazines are no longer popular at all. The police recently started a new campaign against them. I.P.

COMPARATIVE STUDY OF COMICS : AMERICAN AND JAPANESE* — Sazae-san and Blondie

by Taihei Imamura

The purpose of this paper is to compare the character of two heroines in newspaper comics in two different cultures. Sazae-san and Blondie are ideal-typical women of each culture, and both are very popular.

Blondie, created by Chick Young and said to be the most popular comic in the United States, has run for 16 years. It is published in 9,000 newspapers and read by forty million people. This popularity is, perhaps, because *Blondie* is representative of the life of the general run of the American people. The American people may be seeing their own lives in *Blondie.* In a word, *Blondie* is a self-portrait to the American people.

The Bumstead family lives in a suburb of an American city, and Dagwood goes to work daily. Every morning he is hurried by Blondie with only three minutes to catch the bus. Sometimes he misses the bus, and sometimes he changes his clothes in the bus.

---

* Published in the *Me* magazine, Feb. 1953, No. 2. The first section of this article (discussion of Blondie) was abridged by the translator with the permission of the author.

(socks)

Isn't it nice.

Why !

She is studying mathematics now.

Dagwood, who has worked for the same company the whole time, repeats this every morning. Despite steady effort his economic status does not change much. The first characteristic of the humor in *Blondie* is that it relates, more or less, to the frugal family budget of the Bumsteads. Blondie asks Dagwood what he wishes for supper; he, while cleaning his pipe, does not give any definite reply. It is clear that he is calculating the expense. Then Blondie

It's getting warmer.
Would be nice if I could
make a trip.

Oh !

I envy you.

Not fixed yet?
It doesn't work at all.

fluently recites the price list of meats: "Steak is 85¢ a pound, a chicken $2.50, ham $1.20, and lamb 75¢." After listening to this report, Dagwood finally says with a strange smile, "Let's join the vegetarians."

One day Alexander asks his mother for ice cream money, but Blondie tells him that he had better ask his father; however, Dagwood answers him, "Ask your mother." Again he comes to Blondie and she gives the same sugges-

Go playing is popular among ladies, you know.

Well, we can cook once in a while.

Your soup will get cold. You must hurry up. We'll finish the game soon, wait a minute please.

Now, you know what we experience every day.

tion. Finally, Alexander gives up the ice cream and tells his friends, "Someday I want to write a book on the psychology of parents."

Blondie has many things she wants to buy. She is especially careful choosing her hats every year. Blondie and Dagwood cannot agree on hats. So Blondie must devise various tactics to obtain the hat she wants.

For instance, when she liked a hat priced at $8, she

This is the telecasting of
flowers of the Spring.

Now you see cherry blossoms
of Shimoda.....

What !
Cherry blossoms already !

Sale !
Winter clothes reduced !

borrowed two hats priced at $6 and $3 from the store and
showed them to Dagwood. She switched the price tags and
asked him, "Which do you like better?" Dagwood answered, "I like the $3 one," but it is obvious that his judg-
ment is economic, not aesthetic. Then Blondie tells her
husband the truth, that the one which Dagwood liked was
actually $6.

Dagwood becomes sad and considers his next strategem.

Watch your pin !

Oh, thank you very much.

He declares that he has changed his mind and tells her that he likes the other hat.   Blondie kisses him and says, "You mean I can get both of them?   Wonderful."

In this devious way, she gets $9 from her husband and can buy the $8 hat, and pay $1 back to Dagwood.   He is delighted to get the change.

One of the most luxurious events for them is to go out to dinner in a restaurant, but that is a rather expensive

It will rain today.

No, it won't.

You must take your
    umbrella.

No!

At last, I won.

undertaking. One day, as usual, Blondie proposes to go to
a restaurant saying that their two children are also eager
to go. Dagwood replies that with five of their dogs, his side
is the majority.

In spite of their hard daily work, their life is not as
wealthy as we tend to imagine. They have to worry about
the price of meats, think about the allowance for their
children, hesitate to buy a hat or go to a restaurant. It

is a frugal life, and, no doubt, one basis for sympathy with *Blondie* is the careful economy of the American middle class. According to U.S. Bureau of Labor Statistics, a husband when he earns $3,000 a year can buy a new overcoat every seven years. Such households can spare only small amounts of money for educational and recreational purposes.

Another element of humor in *Blondie* is the fact that Dagwood is described as a lucky American who at least has a job. The Bumstead family is happy though they are not rich. The happiness of the family is emphasized by three contrasting themes, namely, (1) Mr. Dithers, Dagwood's boss; (2) tramps who beg for a cup of coffee at the Bumstead's door; and (3) a very aggressive salesman.

Mr. Dithers, who has employed Dagwood for over ten years, seems to be a good natured person, but after each episode with Dagwood, his favorite phrase is "Dagwood! You're fired". With this scream of Mr. Dithers, Dagwood jumps up and reports sadly to his wife, "Everything is over." This conditioned reflex of Dagwood's is well understood by people in a capitalistic society. Mr. Dithers' simple statement impresses on Dagwood the happiness of being employed.

Often Dagwood is troubled by tramps and salesmen. The more forceful a salesman and the more miserable a tramp, the more the happiness of the Bumstead family is emphasized.

The Bumstead family is always happy and gay despite these problems, because their life is stable as long as Dagwood does not lose his job. However, that is not the only reason why the Bumsteads seem to be happy. There is another element to it.

The gay atmosphere of *Blondie* is due to the fact that the behavior of Blondie and Dagwood is that of marionettes rather than humans. Even the most skillfully created marionette cannot do its own thinking. Blondie and Dagwood are like marionettes in that they lack the ability to think.

Blondie is a typical good wife and mother. Like most American women, she is busy keeping house and works hard. She is more cautious than her husband and she takes care of him. But her hard work confines her at home and she can direct her attention only to her housekeeping. To be a good wife and mother, for Blondie, means to be isolated from society and to think about it little. She can recite the price list of meats, but she cannot delibrate about the society in which she is living. In this respect Blondie has something in common with Japanese women. The development of Blondie does not mean the development of her thought, but the development of her skill and technique in cooking, toilette, and handling her husband. She shows only the development of growth of *techniques,* and not of *thought.*

Blondie's thinking does not develop and that is why Blondie is merely a marionette. Her expression is like that of a mechanical marionette in a show-window. She is a domestic marionette who repeats the same behavior every day for her husband. The optimism of Blondie comes from her thoughtlessness and her marionette-like character.

Her husband, Dagwood, also is a marionette who repeats the same behavior every day. His brain is tired out; what he likes best is sleeping. He is absent-minded most of the time when he is at home. He comes home to seek a place to sleep. On Sundays he naps on the sofa of his living room.

Dagwood's second favorite activity is eating. He takes huge sandwiches even after going to bed.

Aside from sleeping and eating, he has domestic tasks like painting his house, repairing the roof, gathering firewood, training and washing his dogs. His reading is limited to either newspapers or detective stories.

In a word, Dagwood Bumstead also is a man who does not think. He resembles his dogs, while Blondie resembles a doll in a show-window. He resembles a dog first because his favorite pleasures are sleeping and eating, and second because he likes to do meaningless things such as fighting with a cat, or receiving a doughnut from Blondie on his nose.

He is an example of a man whom mechnical and hard daily work has deprived of the power of thought. It is a tragedy. In spite of this tragedy, Blondie is full of optimism and the Bumstead family is happy. This is because, though they are not rich, they can enjoy life as long as Dagwood has a job, and they are satisfied with a monotonous middle-class life. Blondie, who represents the American middle-class, defines the nature of their happiness as follows:

"Dagwood, you have a nice job, good wife, children. And you have the latest fountain pen with a life-time guarantee too."

The Japanese comic which is comparable to *Blondie* is *Sazae-san* (Mrs. Sazae) created by Machiko Hasegawa. *Sazae-san* is published in the *Asahi* Newspaper, and she is a familiar figure to millions of Japanese readers.

Like the Bumstead family, Sazae-san's family belongs to the middle-middle class. But the humor of Sazae-san is based largely on the fact that the family while still having the norms of the middle class is not what it used to be economically. Mrs. Sazae Isono, our heroine, lives in a house with a gate.* Due to financial difficulties, however, she decides to do home work and puts a sign at the entrance of her house reading "Sewing." The four members of the Bumstead household can be supported entirely by Dagwood's income, but this Japanese family cannot live on the income of her husband and her father, both of whom are working for a company.**

---

* Having a gate means an economically stable middle class status.
** Sazae-san lives with her husband parents and siblings all together in the same house. It may be an interesting contrast for the reader that while the family size of Blondie is typically American (husband, wife, son, and daughter), Sazae-san's family is a two-generation family, which is typically Japanese. In Sazae-san comics, at least the same amount of emphasis is put on parent-daughter relationships as on husband-wife relationships. (The translator.)

Soon after Sazae-san posts the signboard, a man comes in saying "I understand you do sewing." Both Sazae-san and her mother, delighted to have a customer, say "Yes, of course. I have many customers so you can trust my skill." But the man answers, "I'm from the income tax office."

In her house there is a drawing room furnished with Western furniture. One day a friend visits her. She and her friend were enjoying phonograph records of Chopin and similar composers in the drawing room. Meanwhile, Wakame, her younger sister, five or six years old, comes in and tells her that Mother is calling her. While Sazae-san is out of the room the younger sister plays records for the visitor, but the records are children's songs. Then Sazae-san's younger brother, about twelve years old, comes in. Telling his sister that the music she is playing is not for adults, he takes over the entertainment of the guest. But this time the record played by him is that of "Naniwa-bushi" the most vulgar type of Japanese story. Though Sazae-san does not know what her siblings are doing, the reader of the comic feels amused because he can imagine the embarrassment of Sazae-san. The humor comes from the fact that Sazae-san's middle class sophistication is being seriously compromised by the behavior of her younger siblings.

Like most of the petit-bourgeoisie of Japan, the household of Sazae-san is declining. But even in the midst of this decline they still stick to the manners of a good family. It is an idealistic effort to preserve the manners and etiquette of their former days.

One day, when Katsuo, her younger brother, is reading a book lying on the floor, Sazae-san comes in and says, "I will tell your father about your misbehavior." But at the same moment, the father is being scolded by his wife for reading a book in the bathroom.

One hot summer day when her mother is cooling herself with a fan, the younger sister comes in almost naked. The mother is surprised and calls to Sazae-san saying, "Sazae, please see that your younger sister gets properly dressed." With this remark, however, Sazae-san comes in also wearing just a slip to ask what her mother said.

Another time an uncle of her husband's comes to visit the family. While preparing tea, Sazae-san tells her mother that she has heard that the uncle is almost deaf. The mother brings a cup of tea to the man and begins conversation very politely. Meanwhile Sazae-san asks her mother from the next room, "Shall I bring yokan?" (a sweet bean cake which is considered the most luxurious tea cake.) Her mother answers, "No you needn't. Some potatoes will do." However, when the hostess loudly asks the guest, "I suppose you have difficulty hearing", the answer is, "I think you misunderstand. My wife cannot hear well, but I can." Thus both Sazae-san and her mother are embarrassed.

Sazae-san once came home and rushed into the kitchen. She could not find her rice cake. Both her younger sister and brother are called by her and loudly accused. She does not know that in the living room her voice is being heard by her mother and a guest to whom her rice cake has been served.

Thus the humor in *Sazae-san* arises from the contradiction between the ideology and the actual life of a middle-class family. Their manners become amusing when they have lost their former economic status. Sazae-san is the more humorous because she is not conscious of the contradiction. Moreover, the humor is further accentuated by the forward personality of Sazae-san.

When a visitor who missed her father leaves saying "Please give him my best wishes when he returns," Sazae-san answers very politely, "Yes I will Mr.—" with the utmost courtesy. But a moment later, when the guest comes back to ask the telephone number, Sazae-san is eating the rice-cake which she had served for him.

Certainly Sazae-san is not an old type of Japanese

woman. While Blondie is a type who has appeared following the flapper type of the 20's, Sazae-san is a woman who kicked out the traditional Japanese women. Sazae-san is a new figure of post-war Japan. However, her active and forward behavior is not social action but rather an expression of her personal temperament. Most active Japanese women are not consciously striving to overcome the old behavior patterns.

In a word, the activeness of Sazae-san is activeness for its own sake and not socially purposive. While this vivacity of Sazae-san's is not social but temperamental, it is still her most distinctive trait.

One day, Sazae-san goes to a restaurant with her younger brother and sister and orders three cups of sweet bean soup, but the serving is delayed. Then suddenly all three together shout loudly, "Three cups of bean soup." A man in the next booth stands up and says to the waitress "Serve their order promptly." But the man says later in a low voice to his friend, "That strange noise disturbed our conversation."

Another time, Sazae-san takes a seat in a street car between two men. The man on her left talks to the man on her right. "Shall we have a drink somewhere?", but the man on the right cannot hear him. Again the man on the left says the same thing, but his friend misses the words again. Then Sazae-san, between the two, repeats loudly to the man on the right, "SHALL WE HAVE A DRINK SOMEWHERE?". All the passengers are startled and stare at her. She becomes aware of her strange behavior, becoming suddenly very still, like a Buddha.

Her activeness does not represent rationality, but rather its loss. As drunkenness makes men active, the lack of rational thinking makes contemporary women active. When she is most active she also is most non-rational. Sazae-san's activity seems hysterical. This hysteric response is related to the feudalistic suppression of Japanese women. Feudalistic ways of thinking, combined with middle-class ideology are clearly present in Sazae-san, as illustrated in the next story.

One day Sazae-san is working in her garden wearing dirty working clothes. A professional photographer passes by and feels inspired by the sight of the young housewife at work. He cries out, "Please let me take your picture. I want it for my exhibition!" However, when he brings his camera, he is completely disappointed for Sazae-san has changed her clothes and dressed up in a traditional kimono.

As I mentioned before, Sazae-san's activeness is personal and temperamental. Her family background is a factor in it. Both her father and mother seem to be easy going liberal persons. One day, when the father is comfortably taking a bath, someone rings the bell. He hurriedly dons his bathrobe and goes to the door, where he finds his wife laughing; "Ha ha, you are trapped." Sazae-san's mother is already over fifty, but she still enjoys this kind of humor. She would have enjoyed the life of the middle class before the war.

Her father likes to have a drink before supper. He sings the songs which he learned in his middle-school days. He has his hair peacefully cut by his daughter. These scenes show not only Sazae-san's peaceful family life, but also the fact that her parents lived a "Haikara" (High collar) life before the war when the life of the white collar class was happier and gayer.

Her parents lived most of their lives in the period when the Japanese petit bourgeoisie were most stable and when liberalism in Japan reached its climax (1920-30's). They cannot adjust themselves to the post-war society.

Sazae-san was brought up as the eldest daughter of this family. Her activeness was the result of the liberal training she received from her parents. However, while her activeness was acquired in a relatively prosperous family in the past, in the post-war years she was forced to use it to ward off poverty. Her tasks included going to the countryside to buy vegetables, cultivating her garden, taking care of her siblings, getting rations, and so on. In a word, she is the protector of her family.

Sazae-san's activeness reflects the tremendous changes in Japanese women which took place after the war. In this respect Blondie and Sazae-san are in contrast. Sazae-san is dynamic while Blondie spends most of her time housekeeping. Though Sazae-san also works mainly in her home, her action-area is wider than Blondie's. That is the necessary result of the war and of post-war years. In the immediate post-war years, Japanese women had to line up for hours for rations, and they had to go to the provinces by train to obtain rice, potatoes, and vegetables. They also had to compete with men in order to board the crowded trains. If a woman confined herself to her home, it meant starvation for her family.

The liberation of women in the United States took place some thirty years ago. But the liberation of women in Japan is in its beginnings. Furthermore, this movement went on in the midst of economic destruction caused by war. Japanese women are now getting what American women got three decades ago. This social background, may be the basis for the relative activeness of Sazae-san as compared with Blondie.

Sazae-san having won her freedom only recently, is full of curiosity about everything she experiences. She warns a student riding on the forbidden part of a train, or she makes a sign board which reads, "ATTENTION! Typhoon coming" immediately after hearing the weather forecast on the radio and brings it to the park.

Many people are crowded in front of a beauty shop one day to see a girl whose hair was burned by the hair dresser's error. Sazae-san passes by and makes the people line up to see the girl.

When she asks a policeman the location of a certain street, she does not forget to ask another question of him: "By the way, will you tell me how you are living on your present salary?"

The activeness of Sazae-san may be the vitality of Japanese women in transition. In this sense her behavior has a social significance. However, this does not imply that she is socially conscious. This comic presents the socially neutral petit bourgeoisie. Both static Blondie and dynamic Sazae-san are completely unmindful of the societies in which they are living. The bite of satire is not found in either *Blondie* or *Sazae-san*. The laughter aroused by these comics is slap-stick, and an expression of social neutrality.

The foregoing Sazae-san cartoons are reproduced through the special permission of Hasegawa Machiko and the *Asahi Shimbun*.

CHILDREN'S COMICS
IN JAPAN

by Kanji Hatano

I. STEREOTYPES IN JAPANESE CHILDREN'S COMICS

In the year 1955, as a result of severe competition, children's magazines began giving comic books as gifts to their readers. This gift-giving system is not new, but until recently the gifts were such toys as a telescope or sling shot. Now, instead of toys, the gifts are two or three comic books of 32 to 60 pages each. Since, in addition to the gift comics, there are several serial comics published in each magazine, the reader is exposed to over ten kinds of comics every month. The P.T.A., the Women's Union, and other organizations are watching this tendency closely, and a movement for the elimination of harmful books has begun.

As a result of this movement, the stereotypes in comics are changing. For example, until a year ago, the treatment of the hero in Judo and classical comics was an imitation of Western comics; e.g. a beautiful princess is saved by a skillful fencer.

However, in the comics of 1955, there are almost no female characters. The plot has changed in such a way that a hero develops his skill and/or personality through a series of contests finally attaining championship. We

may call this kind of comic in which the hero develops
women go three decades ago. This social background
upward "developmental". The developmental comic itself
is not new. From 1929 through 1935, the most popular
comic hero was Nora-kuro, a "stray-dog" type who eventually entered military service and succeeded in reaching
the rank of captain. The comic was adapted in book form
and called *Nora-kuro, P.F.C., Nora-kuro, Sergeant, Nora-kuro, Lieutenant,* and so on. This established the prototype of what we have called developmental comics.

The Nora-kuro series was very popular because it functioned to transform a child's inferiority complex into a
desire to improve and it was suitable to a period of
militarism.

Since 1954, we can observe the reappearance of developmental comics. Although there is no such clearly defined
system of rank as there was in Nora-kuro, the Judo,
wrestling, and other action comics still foster high aspirations whose final goal is becoming a champion. The upward
aspiration, of course, indicates a child's admiration for
adults.

Before 1955, some judo comics portrayed a boy Judoist
as more skillful than an adult Judoist. This theme was
welcome to younger readers in Japanese society, where
children are so suppressed by adults. However, this theme
has now practically disappeared, for during the movement
to abolish harmful books, there were complaints that it
"treats adults with contempt."

II.   A SURVEY OF COMIC PUBLICATIONS

There are three kinds of comics for Japanese children.
The first consists of serial comics in boys' and girls' magazines, including some intended essentially for 5th and
6th grade primary school children (11 and 12 years
old). Among these, such magazines as *Fifth Grade, Boys'*

Club, Girls' Club, Adventure Boys, and *Boys' Comics,* have a combined circulation of over 500,000 copies. Approximately one-third of the space of these magazines is devoted to comics.

The second group includes comic books, which usually have a first printing of 5,000 to 10,000 copies. About half of them will go out of print after that, and the other half will continue on to second or third printings. These books can be obtained from retail book stores, and their price varies between 100 and 200 yen (28¢ to 56¢).

The third type consists of cheap comic books which children obtain from toy shops and *Zokki* book stores. A *Zokki* store was originally a bargain book store which specialized in the sale of publishers' remainders at 70% to 80% off list price. However, nowadays, the *Zokki* stores are the primary market for cheap publications. There are approximately 1000 *Zokki* shops and about 5000 toy shops in Japan. The comic books they handle are printed in first editions of 5,000 to 30,000 copies. The prices vary from 25 to 60 yen, with two or three sometimes sold together for 50 yen. Characteristically these third class comics lack originality in art work, the paper is cheap, the colors are poor, and the printing is not clear. The size of the magazines is usually about half that of American comics. However, they are the most popular comics, and over 1,000 different books are produced annually. There is no weekly comic serial publication in Japan. All the children's magazines are monthlies.

III. CHILDREN'S BEHAVIOR WITH REGARD TO COMICS

1) *Children in an Urban Setting:*

In November 1955, we undertook a survey of children's comic reading at a typical big city primary school (Miyamae primary school, Arakawa, Tokyo). Our first finding was that comic books and magazines function as a sort of currency. That is, children exchange comics among each other.

The percentage of children who use comics as their major reading source decreases from the fourth to the sixth grade. The rate is shown in the following table.

Children Using Comics As Their Major Reading Source

	3rd grade	4th	5th	6th
Boys	65%	71%	70%	57%
Girls	74%	85%	68%	45%

It is clear from this chart that comics are the spiritual "main course" for two thirds of all children up to the 5th grade, and it is after they reach the 6th grade that they become more interested in other reading materials. This finding is confirmed by the answers to the question, "Do you like comics?" While 70% of 3rd grade children answered, "Yes" to this question, only 35% of boys and 26% of girls in the 6th grade answered the same. Furthermore, 18% of 6th grade children said that they "dislike" comics.

The 20 comics named most often as most popular grouped as follows:

Life comics	6
Judo comics	5
Classical comics	4
Story comics	3
Adventure and detective comics	2
	——
	20

Judo and Classical (historical stories whose main theme is fencing) are favorites; they are the equivalents of Western comics in the United States.

The following table indicates how the children in the urban school obtained comic books.

	3rd grade	4th	5th	6th
Ask parents to buy	18%	22%	18%	21%
With one's own allowance	14%	12%	9%	7%
Borrow from friends	16%	38%	46%	48%
Borrow from library	22%	5%	11%	10%
Borrow from rental bookstore	30%	23%	16%	14%
	100%	100%	100%	100%

The percentage of children who ask their parents to buy comics is almost the same from the 3rd through the 6th grade; and the percentage of those who borrow from friends increases with the years. On the other hand, borrowing from rental bookstores and buying with an allowance decreases as the children grow up. As they become older, they become interested in buying other things.

2) Children in a rural setting:

The same questionnaire and method which we used in Tokyo was adopted in November 1955 with rural children at Hotohara Primary School, Sukagawa, Fukushima prefecture. 95% of the population there are farmers.

The percentage of rural children who use comics as their major reading matter is shown in the following chart.

	3rd grade	4th	5th	6th
Boys	80%	100%	60%	70%
Girls	84%	88%	78%	57%

It is evident from this chart that the penetration of comics into children's culture is greater in the rural community than it was in the urban. The extreme case is that of 4th grade boys. The decrease in comic reading by the 6th grade is less for rural than for urban children. While 57% of 6th grade boys in the Tokyo sample use comics for their major reading, 70% of the 6th grade boys in this village do. This indicates a relative lack of cultural facilities in rural communities which can ultimately provide a substitute for comics.

"Do You Like Comics?"

	3rd grade		4th grade		5th grade		6th grade	
	Boys	Girls	Boys	Girls	Boys	Girls	Boys	Girls
Like	80%	84%	100%	88%	100%	83%	71%	64%
Dislike	0	8	0	0	0	0	6	0
No Answer	20	8	0	12	0	17	23	36

It is worth noting that the trend away from liking comics which was clearly observed among children in the city, is weak in our rural sample. The rural children obtained their comics in the following ways:

	3rd grade	4th	5th	6th
Ask parent to buy	34%	31%	16%	12%
With one' own allowance	4	0	6	2
Borrow from friends	23	38	33	37
Borrow from library	35	31	40	44
Other sources	4	0	5	5

In contrast to urban children, very few children of this village have the habit of buying comic books with their own allowance or savings. The rate of use of library facilities for comic reading is higher than in the urban community. (There was no rental bookstore in the rural test community.)

Most of Japan's rural areas, despite their pastoral beauty, are culturally underdeveloped and this situation is reflected in the comics-communication behavior of the boys and girls.

A CONTENT ANALYSIS OF POST-WAR JAPANESE POPULAR SONGS[*]

by Hiroshi Minami
and members of the
Institute of Social Psychology

I. THE PROBLEM

The purpose of this study is to ascertain some content characteristics of popular songs in the immediate post-war period which may express or represent the peculiar social situation of Japan at that time. First we shall describe content characteristics of these popular songs. Secondly, by examining the reasons for their achieving popularity, we shall treat problems connected with their method of production. Third we shall show the philosophy of the songs.

II. CONTENTS OF POST-WAR POPULAR SONGS

1) Sampling:

It is impossible and unnecessary to examine all the popular songs published after the war. Since they total several hundred we selected a number of especially *popular* ones, using two criteria:

Akiko Naraki, and Sachiko Tamabe. Later this article was included
No. 2, 1950, by Hiroshi Minami, Kazuo Tatsuno, Hidetoshi Kato,
Akiko Naraki, and Sachiko Tanabe. Later this article was included
(with a little modification) in *Yume to Omokage—Studies in Popular
Arts*.

a)   We sampled the best sellers of the main phonograph record companies, King, Victor, Columbia, Polydor, and Teichiku, in the period August 1945 to December 1948. It is difficult to estimate the *absolute* sales figures of best-sellers, since they are top secrets of the companies. The best-sellers of each company are therefore relative to its size.

b)   We also selected songs which were sung three times or more on the Hit Parade program of N.H.K. (semi-governmental Japanese Broadcasting System). As we shall see later, however, there were some manipulative commercial tactics on the part of record producers behind the selection of songs for this program. The period from which songs were sampled was from December 1948 to December 1949.

Fifty-three songs were chosen from source one, and twenty-three from source two, but since 15 appeared in both lists, the actual sample used totals 61. (Table I lists these songs.)

2)   Classification of Song Content:

Tentatively we classified popular song content according to rather literal themes. In many cases in which more than two themes appear in a song the song is classified by the dominant theme. The following four categories will be used:

a)   Sentimental: introversion, being rejected, being isolated, and so on.

b)   Decadent or nihilist: destructive, often self-destructive.

c)   Romantic: dreamy, hope for uncertain future luck, love, or exotic mood.

d)   Optimistic: so called nonsense songs; often the text is literally meaningless.

Now let us turn to a more detailed analysis of each group.

3) Content Analysis of Each Group:

a) Sentimental category (29 songs)

Twenty-nine out of 61 or nearly half belong to this group. This sentimentality has long been deplored by Japanese critics and intellectuals. In fact sentimentalism is traditionally (at least in recent decades) the dominant theme in Japanese popular songs. What are the elements* which compose this sentimentality? They are: parting, memory, giving up, regret, love, loneliness, feebleness, homesickness, and so on.

Among these 29 songs we can find the element "love" in 22, "memory" in 13, "hope" in 13, "parting" in 10, "regret" in 10, "loneliness" in 10, "giving up" in 8.

Let us now explain the nature of these elements and how they are interrelated to each other.

What is characteristic of "love" in these songs is that there is no positive willingness to make love. In other words it does not mean passionate love but the feeling of love which the heroine or hero still feels after the departure of the loved one. "Parting" and "loneliness" are thus connected with the "love" element. Throughout the 29 songs the men and women are solitary and separated in time or space, or at least psychologically.

Moreover, "love" neither implies active appeals to the lover, nor attempts to overcome the separation. The heroine or hero sings, grieved and pained, about her broken heart and heart-rending sorrow.

> I am crying for you from my loneliness, but the valley echoes only my voice. (55)
> He has left an enduring image in my heart, night after night.
> And I know that he will never come back again. (16)

In this sad love, there is no positive willingness to make love. Instead, negative regret and giving up are the only relations between the two lovers.

---

* Element need not mean word. Some elements appear as sentences.

Sigh and give up, give up and sigh. I cannot give him up though I try. (21)
No one waiting for me, petals are falling down, I must give him up, give him up. (15)
Drinking up a glass of wine, I will give her up, I will cut her from my heart. (5)

Thus he (or she) seems to suceed in giving up his lover, but at the same time there remains the feeling of regret.

Yesterday I gave her up, but today I love her more. Oh, love is a painful scarlet thistle. (1)

Since regret comes with giving up, the men who appear in these songs are ambivalent. They are worried and puzzled by contrary impulses. This ambivalence makes them all the more mad for love.

At th same time the ambivalent feeling is connected with loneliness.

I will give him up, give him up. Oh, anyway I am alone! (15)
Gone all my friends, and I am leaning on a post alone. (57)

The women who appear are descibed as both lonely and also weak and helpless.

Women are weak red flowers, though men never weep. (44)

or

Why did the flower of love come to my maiden mind, though a dream is but a dream. (21)

Sometimes, giving up is connected with a nihilistic mood or the desperation which we shall discuss in the next section. An example is:

I will cut her from my mind, I will give up—at best this is an uncertain world; days are passing with cheap music. (5)

In this case giving up is related to desperation instead of regret. Love, even though it is felt when separated, is a present feeling. However, when the object of love belongs to the past, the feeling becomes "memory." The examples are:

I can't forget the memory, the dear old days. I shall remember as long as I live. (54)
When I think of you by the unforgettable window, the wind whispers to me the song of the past. (55)

As in the case of love, the memory element is always connected with regret or loneliness. However, it must be noted that the content of these memories is always full of joy. The happier the memory of the past, the more

112

miserable and lonely the present. And at the same time, the memory is an escape mechanism from the frustrating present.

The popularity of a popular lyrics writer is more or less determined by his technique in combining these delicate elements.

Among sentimental songs, one will find some which contain the element of "hope."

> Though tomorrow is uncertain, I am hoping for a Blue Bird tomorrow. (59)
> Searching for the happiness that waits beyond the mountain, I am travelling today too. (1)
> With the dream of the young, admiration flies on the sky like heavenly stars. (55)

However, hope, like love, is rather negative and uncertain.

The hope is somewhere beyond man's reach; they admire it in vain. The dream can never be realized. When they compare this hope with reality, giving up or loneliness become important themes closely connected with it. Hope belongs to the future while memory belongs to the past; both of them express the same psychological mechanism, escape.

Now let us turn to classify the 29 sentimental songs by sex. Among the 29, 11 are sung by a man, 9 by a woman, 9 by both. The contents show some difference by sex as to the treatment of the elements of love and parting. Women sing lines like this:

> People have gone away, and I am standing at the train station alone. (57)
> However I wait for him, this is the night he has not yet come, this is the night of loneliness. (15)
> The bitterness of the day when I cannot see you. My flaming heart is like a pitiful flower in the desert.

Sorrow, parting, painful waiting, are frequently found. In a word, static passivity is the symbol of womanhood.

On the contrary, in a man's case, as shown by the following examples, the ideal is to pretend to be happy when he is crying, and to say goodbye decisively, and show tenderness to his girl when they part.

113

Don't ask me more, a sea-man has his own way. (53)
Don't weep, little dove. Oh my dear! Your weeping gives me
unbearable attachment. (29)
Lovely eyes and sweet lips, goodbye, goodbye to all. (50)

b) Decadent or Nihilist category (16 songs)

The second group is composed of songs which can be categorized under decadence. This type has also been typical of Japanese popular songs.

The main characteristic of this group is that the themes are attributed to the specific psychology of the members of specific social (mostly anti-social) groups.

Among 16 songs, (a) 6 are the songs of sailors, (b) 6 of Yakuza (gangsters), (c) 2 of street girls, (d) and 2 others.

Historically, this kind of song originated in the famous *Boatman Song* saying:

I am dead zebra-grass on the river-beach,

which was published in 1923, (the beginning of the depression after World War I). In 1934 there appeared *Akagi Lullaby* and *This is Just Sailors' Love,* both of which clearly represent a decadent tendency. And this tendency has continued until the present. Comparing these classic decadent songs with those of nowadays, we find the style and content remain quite the same.

The elements which characterize this group are as follows: travelling away -10, self-insult and desperation -9, obstinacy -6, self-praise -3, giving up, and loneliness. We noted in the preceding section that parting is one of the most important elements of sentimentalism. Here again travelling away is the dominant theme in the group. Nihilistic wanderers, such as sailors whose future fate is uncertain, or gamblers expelled from their hometown, are the heroes of this category.

First, let us analyse sailors' songs. The song *This is Just Sailors' Love* of 1934 is, as we mentioned before, the origin of the sailor song. Originally, the term sailor had

114

a rather romantic and even exotic connotation, but as time went on the connotation changed. Nowadays, the ideal type of a sailor is a man who is living in a "dark town" and who appears in the harbor at midnight, under starless skies, etc.

In these six songs almost identical syntax is used.

> Don't weep, lovely eyes, at best I am a sailor whose fate is uncercertain. (25)
> Lamps are red in blue night fog, anyway I am a lonely guy. (56)
> I may indulge myself in wine and women, anyway at best I am a lonely sailor. (51)

"Anyway" or "at best," these self-hating desperate expressions often connected with a social inferiority complex, constitute the self-insult element.

Sometimes, the self-insult based on an inferiority complex takes the form of a reaction formation, i.e., self-praise like

> Saying nothing, just pretending to smile. Ah, this is the very man of men. (56)

The next theme concerns Yakuza gangsters, who also also represent the dark side of society.* However, while sailors represent the outcasts of modern or contemporary society, Yakuza songs express feudalistic ways of life. Self-praise among Yakuza is well justified in terms of *Girl, Ninjo,*** or feudalistic norms.

> I do not care to leave Akagi, but I am attached to the men. To toast this man of obstinacy, let's have a cup of the water of this unforgettable mountain. (40)
> Shall I live in love? or shall I live in a manly way? Oh this floating world is a bitter place because of Giri. (61)

Such inhuman agony is regarded as heroic in these songs. The Yakuza share feelings of inferiority with the sailors;

> I know not where I die; I am a Yakuza man kicked out of the ordinary world. (34)
> It may be obstinacy or manly pride. Whatever it is, I am a lonely outcast. (10)

---

* "Yakuza" means a gambler-gangster of the feudal age, especially the late Tokugawa period. Sometimes (at least in popular fiction) they were the friends of exploited farmers. As to the details, see: *A Study in Yakuza Fiction*, by Michitaro Tada in this volume.
** "Giri" and "Ninjo" norms are well discussed in Ruth Benedict's *Chrysanthemum and the Sword*.

115

It should be noted that Yakuza songs are, in a sense, the contemporary form of *Naniwabushi*,* a traditional narrative type of story telling.

Last in this group, we shall discuss the songs of prostites.** The street-girls, called *pan-pan* girls by the G.I.'s, are a postwar social group. Songs expressing women's feelings of being outcast, however, can also be found before the war. *Song of a Bar-Waitress* of 1931, and *Life in a Back Street* of 1938 are pioneers in this category.

The street-girls' songs are characterized by self-insult and sentiment. In the case of male outcasts, there is a kind of pride, expressed by such phrases as "this is the very man of men," but female outcasts, express neither pride nor pretension. Their womanhood is symbolized by complete helplessness and hopelessness.

> Reading my fate by a shooting star, I know not where tonight's bed is. Crying after drying, my tears have already dried up (11) Smiling with lipstick, crying in the cold night wind. Don't fool me. Anyway, all that I have is a hopeless dream. (19) How sad it is, this is the place called hell. (19)

Sometimes this feeling becomes rather masochistic.

> Who made me such a girl? (11)

At the same time there is a kind of pride in saying, "I am a beautiful night flower of Tokyo."

c) *Romantic category* (10 songs)

The elements which characterize this group are, admiration -5, love -4, exoticism -3, urbanism -3. In this group, there are no such elements as "sad" and "lonely" which were dominant in the two categories discussed before. Instead, the general atmosphere is bright and romantic.

---

* Naniwabushi is story-telling with songs accompanied by a Shamisen, a three-stringed guitar-like instrument. Most of the stories are those of Yakuza and Samurai. This type of story-telling is still broadcast over the radio networks and has a following among farmers.
** After the war, the number of street-walkers rapidly increased and many novels and dramas were written about them. They were familiar figures in post-war Japan. [Previously in Japan prostitution was licensed but confined indoors.]

In category (1) hope was passive, related to giving up; in this category it is positive and active. The object: admiration of love, admiration of foreign countries, admiration of an unknown girl, or admiration of cities.

> I will love her with all my heart. Bright hope, admiration, twinkling golden stars! (17)
> In the bloom of youth I am passing a hill. The sky is blue and the grass is green. (41)

are examples of admiration for love.

> Oh that white hotel building behind the coconut-trees of Honolulu. (2)
> Rose of the South, you are the very queen of the flowers, you are the lovely rose of Spain. (22)

are examples of exoticism.

> Black eyes, dreamy smile, pretty girl. (28)
> Lovely eyes and dimples, oh flower-girls of Tokyo. (48)

represent a degree of affection for unknown girls.

The treatment of urbanism involves assertions of both the bright and dark sides of urban life, though generally the city is regarded as a place of pleasures.

> Oh dreamy city, Tokyo! (58)
> Bright neon lights, city of love, city of flowers. (49)

are examples.

As is clear from these examples, admiration is the dominant theme in this category. However, it should be pointed out that admiration in the romantic songs is frequently quite unrealistic. In the sentimental songs, we observed that hope was always compared with reality. But in this group, there is no reality-consciousness. Admiration is, in a word, fantasy in a psychological sense.

Another general characteristic of this group is that there is no grammatical subject in these songs.* In category (1), there were subjects such as "You," or "I," and there was also consciousness of definite human relations. But in this group, we do not find these pronouns. In other words, in Japanese popular songs there is "the *sorrow* of *my* love" but not "the *pleasure* of *my* love." Pleasure is always

---

* In the Japanese language, especially in daily conversation, the subject is scarcely mentioned.

abstract, generalized, and ambiguous, and never becomes specific.

d) Nonsense category (6 songs)

The elements which characterize this group are nonsense, ignorance, and easy-goingness, and most of them are comical.   They have relatively little in common with each other, but we can note certain comparisons between the content of recent songs in this category with that of nonsense songs before the war.   First, while pre-war songs had original and unique phrasings (which are, of course, impossible to translate), the postwar nonsense songs are very simple in their content.

> Oh it's funny, ha a it's funny. What's funny? A girl's laughing because she broke her clogs. (1926)

or

> Don't worry about money. We can share the graveyard with the rich people. Whether you cry or smile, you have only one life. (1932)

These pre-war songs are relatively interesting and funny in Japanese.   On the other hand, post-war ones as for instance in the case of *Tokyo Boogie*, have comparatively less content, just repeating simple words such as "let's dance, let's sing, let's laugh."

Secondly, pre-war nonsense songs reflected, more or less, the life orientation of the petite bourgeois, especially that of the white collar class.

> Oh happy payday! Now I would like to have a drink with you. (1936)
> I thought he was busy at the company. However, however,— (he was drinking). (1938)
> However he tries to pretend to be a good husband outside, in fact he is henpecked. It's foolish to say sweet words to the wife, when he spent all his pay for drink. (1938)

Such verses can be sharp and funny.

Pre-war Japanese nonsense songs caricatured the life of the middle class.   Some were explicitly class conscious.

> I am a proletarian, wearing a dirty blue over-all

and

118

The heaven of proletarians, the cheap inn. Oh, my legs are not so bad to sleep with.

We do not find such songs after the war.

After the war, there was a vogue of boogie-woogie. Its appeal was mainly in the gestures of the singers, not in the content of the lyrics.

4) The Analysis of Words:

Now we will turn our attention to an analysis of words used in popular songs. First, as we mentioned before, there are many Japanese popular songs in which grammatical subject and human-relational expressions are very ambiguous. The feelings and thoughts of the hero are expressed indirectly by descriptions of nature.
Examples:

Rain is crying this lonely evening. (8)
A heart is wet under the moonlight. (35)
For whom is a red flower waiting? (21)

Such expressions are, no doubt, based upon a type of traditional Japanese short poem, Haiku.*

The number of nouns thus related to nature and their frequency are as follows: Wind—20, Rain—14, Star—10, Fog, Night fog—14, Sky—7, Wave—6, Sunset—5. Wind is used in a rather sentimental way, such as "chilly wind" (15), "crying wind" (16), or sometimes "lonely wind" (39). Rain also is said in these contexts.

As to nouns, not referring to tangible objects, the frequency is as follows: Dream—38, Night—27, Love—26, Song—17, Heart—17, Man—14, Tonight—11, Soul—10, Illusion—10, Image—9, Regret—8.

"Dream," in most cases is "faint" (23), "cannot be realized" (21), or "of old days" (35). "Night," without exception, is used to describe love scenes. The term "man" was found 14 times, while "woman" was found only 6 times. Most of the "men" are used in phrases like "Man's

---

* Such expression through nature is traditional. This technique is at its extreme in "Haiku" poetry, or three-line, 17-syllable poems.

pride," and "This is the man of men," while women, as we have indicated before, are "lonely" and "weak."

As to pronouns, it was found that indefinite ones were frequent. Who, whose, whom—15; compared to You— 13, I (feminine)—9, I (masculine)—6.

Examples of the context in which the indefinite pronoun is used are:

> For whom are my lips waiting? (14)
> For whom am I waiting? (21)

or

> Who knows my tears? (59)

The term "I alone" was found in 14 cases, while there were 9 cases in which "We two" was used.

Among common nouns: Tear—16, Window—14, Port —11, Hill—9, Eyes—8. Needless to say, it is clear that these are also sentimental symbols.

The frequency of verbs was as follows: Cry—33, Part —20, Think of—12, Pass by—12, Wait—12, Smile—12, Give up—10, Be wet—10, Tremble—10, Go back—9, Embrace—8, Cannot forget—8, Sing—10. Except for "smile," "sing," and "embrace," all of these verbs indicate more or less negative and passive behavior. And in context, even these three seemingly positive verbs are used tragically.

Attention must also be paid to the fact that there are 33 instances of "cry" while there are only 3 of the word "*do not* cry" and 8 instances of "cannot forget" as against 2 of "forget."

Adjectives are: Cute, Pretty—27, Sad—15, Unbearable —14, Dear—14, Lonely—14. Most of "cute" or "pretty" are in references to "pretty girls," in sailor songs, so that it is impossible to say that this term expresses something joyful.

The exclamation "Oh" was found 49 times, a high frequency.

III. PRODUCTION OF POPULAR SONGS

Section II was devoted to a content analysis of popular songs. It is now necessary to examine the method of production of popular songs because this is a factor which may distort the relationship between their content and general social attitudes.

In Japan, most popular songs are produced and advertised by commercial phonograph record companies, so we shall start our investigation with them.

1) Sales:

According to the figures published by the Record Association (June 1948), 47% of record sales are popular songs. As of May 1949, 60% of the 1,300,000 records produced monthly are light music, and 80% of this light music consisted of popular songs. Popular songs thus are just under half of the total output of records.

2) Control:

The production of a popular song is mainly determined by the decision of a director on the staff of a record company, though text writers, composers, and singers are also important. Needless to say, most of the directors think primarily in terms of profit. Some are artistically minded, but they cannot disregard profit.

The usual procedure is to choose a song which presents a minimum of risk; that is to say, to make it as similar as possible to one which has already proved to be a hit.

The Flower-girl series (*Flower-girl of Shanghai, of Tokyo,* etc.) is an example of this policy. Though the director always needs some kind of originality, the power of tradition is also important.

3) Advertisement and other entertainment enterprises:

A popular song is advertised in all possible ways: poster, newspaper, stage-show, radio, and so on. Advertisement through the stage is a post-war phenomenon.

Ironically, it was due to the fact that singers could not live solely on the income from records.

The most important publicity arises from the relationship between the record companies and the movie producers. Before the war, the record companies had priority over the movies; that is, a movie was based on a record which had become popular. Since the war, the relation has been reversed because of inflation. Records are made based on movies which have become popular. However, recent trends show that the pre-war relationship is returning.

Characteristically, movie songs have high popularity for a short period. Almost half of the songs on the "Hit Parade" were movie songs, as were over 30% of post-war popular songs in general.

Another form of publicity is through the N.H.K. radio network. (This was the only radio system in existence when this paper was written, although at present there are also over 50 commercial stations.) Since N.H.K. is noncommercial, the advertising cannot be done openly. Employees of record companies used to send postcards (pretending to be ordinary listeners) requesting the broadcast of their favorite song on the "Hit Parade." This method, of course, distorted the objective selection of songs for the program.

IV. JAPANESE PHILOSOPHY AS EXPRESSED IN POPULAR SONGS

The content of the popular songs may not fully reflect the social psychology of the people, because, as we have seen, there are some factors which distort this reflection. However, our assumption is that there must be some kind of correspondence between the content of mass culture and a people's orientation. The loneliness, helplessness, and similar general themes of Japanese popular songs represent the unfortunate social situation of Japan.

On the assumption that there is such a relationship between mass culture and a people's orientation, we would like to conclude this study with generalizations on the philosophy of Japanese popular songs.

1) *Pessimism:*

Japanese songs generally lack completeness. They continually repeat such themes as "giving up" and "parting." They sell tragic tears. They contain scarcely any sense of creativeness and productivity. This tendency may be defined as pessimism.

2) *Fatalism:*

There were many expressions such as "at best" or "anyway." These refer to some kind of super-human power which controls the world. The assumption of the existence of this outside power, beyond the reach of human beings, leads to fatalism.

3) *Existentialism:*

The Japanese do not express their agony and loneliness on a behavioral level. Instead they internalize their helplessness and keep it in mind. Psychoanalytically, according to Jung, the Japanese may be introverts and philosophically, this attitude can be defined as a variant of existentialism.

4) *Pre-modern Patterns of Impulse Expression:* *

Some songs still express *giri* and *ninjo,* feudal social norms. Expression of human impulses is patterned by these pre-modern social norms.

---

* "Pre-modern patterns of impulse expression" refers essentially to "ninjo." She Ruth Benedict, *Chrysanthemum and the Sword,* Chapter 9.

Table 1

No.	Grouping	Original Title	Translation
1	I	Ai no hokage	Light of Love
2	III	Akogare no Hawaii Koro	Voyage to Hawaii of Our Dreams
3	II	Chuji Komoriuta	Chuji Lullaby
4	III	Ginza no Ame	The Rain of the Ginza
5	I	Haha Kobai	Red Plum Mother
6	II	Hanauta Dochu	Travel Humming
7	IV	Hanauta Kaido	Humming Highway
8	I	Hashi no tamotono Kissaten	Teahouse by the Bridge
9	IV	Hey-Hey Boogie	Hey-Hey Boogie
10	II	Hitori tabi	Travelling Alone
11	II	Hoshi no nagareni	With a Shooting Star
12	I	Ikoku no Oka	Foreign Hills
13	II	Kaeri bune	Returning Boat
14	I	Kanashiki Takebue	Sorrowful Bamboo-Flute
15	I	Kimi mate domo	Though I Am Waiting for You
16	I	Kimi wasureji no burusu	Forget-You-Not Blues
17	III	Kirameku seiza	Twinkling Stars
18	I	Kiri no minato ni Hi ga urumu	Wet Lights in a Foggy Harbor
19	II	Kiri no nagare ni	Under the Fog
20	I	Kobanzame no uta	Song of the Golden Shark
21	I	Kao no Manjushage	Love Song of Manjusaka
22	III	Minami no bara	Rose of the South
23	I	Minato ga mieru oka	Harbor over the Hill
24	II	Minato ni akai hi ga tomoru	Red Lamps in the Harbor
25	II	Minato shanson	Harbor Chanson
26	I	Nagare no tabiji	Wandering Travel
27	I	Nagasaki ereji	Nagasaki Elegy
28	III	Nagasaki no zabon uri	Pomelo Seller of Nagasaki
29	I	Nakuna kobato yo	Don't Cry Little Dove
30	I	Namida no komadori	Weeping Robin
31	I	Natsukashi no burusu	My Dear Blues
32	II	Odori tsukarete	Weary of Dancing
33	IV	Orizuru kaido	The Paper Crane's Road
34	II	Oshidori Dochu	Travelling as a Couple
35	I	Otoko ippiki no uta	Song of a Real Man
36	II	Otoko muho Matsu	Bad Man, Matsu
37	I	Reijin no uta	Song of the Beauty
38	IV	Ringo no uta	Apple Song
39	I	365 ya	365 Nights
40	II	Saraba Akagi yo	Goodbye, Mt. Akagi
41	III	Seishun paradaisu	Youth Paradise
42	III	Shanghai no Hanauri-musume	Flower Girl of Shanghai
43	I	Siberia ereji	Siberian Elegy

124

44	I	Shin Aizenkatsura	The New Beloved Judas-Tree
45	IV	Tanko Bushi	Miner's Song
46	I	Tareka yume naki	Is There Anyone without His Dream?
47	IV	Tokyo Boogie Woogie	Tokyo Boogie Woogie
48	III	Tokyo no hanauri musume	Flower Girl of Tokyo
49	III	Tokyo no yoru	Night of Tokyo
50	I	Tokyo yo Sayonara	Goodbye Tokyo
51	II	Tomari bune	The Staying Boat
52	I	Tsukiyori no shisha	A Messenger from the Moon
53	II	Wakare no defune	The Parting Boat
54	I	Wakaretemo	Even After Parting
55	I	Yamagoya no tomoshibi	Lights in a Mountain Hut
56	II	Yogiri no burusu	Blues of the Foggy Night
57	I	Yoru no platform	Night Platform
58	III	Yume awaki Tokyo	Faint Dream of Tokyo
59	I	Yume yo moichido	Come Back My Dream Again
60	I	Yunomachi ereji	Hot Springs Resort Elegy
61	II	Zundoko bushi	Zundoko Song*

* "Zundoko" is a shout to mark time.

A SURVEY OF POSTWAR JAPANESE MOVIES*

by Hiroshi Minami

One of the most influential mass media in contemporary Japan is the film. The aim of this paper is to summarize briefly the content, characteristics, audience, and effect of the movies shown in Japan in the period after the War.

1. THE CONTENT

A. Japanese Movies:

After the War the content of Japanese movies showed the following trends:

a) *Decrease of historical** movies*—596 movies were produced in the period from August 1945 to 1950. Table I shows the proportion of historical and contemporary films among them. It is clear from the Table that the proportion of historical movies decreased considerably from what it had been in the preceding 15 years.

---

* First published in the *Shiso* magazine, August 1951, No. 326.
** "Historical" and "contemporary"—is the most common thematic classification used by students of movies. The former deal with such themes as *Samurai* or *Yakuza*, both of which are feudal characters. In a sense these are the equivalent of American Western movies, for fighting scenes are their main attraction. The latter are movies whose themes are taken from present day life.

Table I
Thematic Classification of Japanese Movies*

Year	Historical	Contemporary	Total
1931 - July 1945	2964 (53%)	2580 (47%)	5544
August 1945 - 1950	84 (14%)	512 (86%)	596

However, one cannot say that the dominance of the themes found in historical films has ended altogether, for two elements of the historical films—namely action and feudalistic ideology—remain alive in disguise in some contemporary films. The vitality of the historical film is well demonstrated by the fact that they began returning when supervision by the American Occupation authorities became more tolerant.**

b) Increase of crime movies—The aggressiveness and action of historical movies was supplied partly by American movies and partly by Japanese crime movies. Crime themes are hardly found among prewar films, but 23% of postwar films are of crime and gangsters. These movies directly or indirectly treat criminals as heroes.

c) Patterns of love—With few exceptions, every movie has some love element. Since the war this element is of growing importance. 25% of postwar films are specifically called love stories. However, like Japanese democracy, the liberation of love on the screen is incomplete.

Love in Japanese movies has the following characteristics:

(1) 90% of loves in the movies are triangular.

(2) The ending of these triangular loves is mostly determined by the status of the hero or heroine. Those who are of low and poor status lose or give up their love: The sorrow of love is a typical theme of Japanese movies.

(3) Occupation is the symbol which indicates status. The

---

*   Data from Japan Movie Association 1950.
** Immediately after the Occupation began, the Occupation Forces Prohibited the production of movies which contained feudalistic morals. By the time of writing (1951), the policy had changed and the control of the content had become much looser.

most popular occupations are doctor and nurse. Next comes artist, followed by journalist.

(4) Several films contain the theme of extramarital love by wives seeking for liberation from feudalistic norms. This theme is specifically postwar. The motivation of most of these heroines is no more than fickleness and sometimes they have to renounce their lovers.

In the movies at least, Japanese love is still based on traditional values.

d) Family characteristics—17% of the movies produced in the year 1950 describe conflicts in a family or similar primary group. Typical of this kind of film are the mother movies.* These conficts are not permitted to be solved in the films by the disorganization of the traditional family. The ideal which is portrayed is that of a person who sacrifices himself (or herself) to preserve the established familial order.

If we regard family relation films and crime films as contemporary forms of two elements of the historical films, then we get a considerably different picture of the content emphasis in postwar films. This is shown in Table II.

Table II
Content of Postwar Japanese Movies (1950)

Family relation	17%)
Crime	23%)
Historical	14%)
Others	46%)

Note: The total of "Family", "Crime", and "Historical" films is 54% which is identical with the figure of prewar historical films. See Table I.

---

* Mother movies (*Haha mono*) form a series of tragedies in which a mother suffers for the happiness of her child. *Haha Kobai* in the list of popular songs studied in this volume, is a song originating in a movie of the same title, which is one of the mother movies.

128

B. *American Movies:*

Table III indicates the dominance of American movies around the world, but also the low proportion of American movies in Japan. However, when we take the American influence on all aspects of Japanese culture into consideration, American impact on the Japanese movie world is substantial.

Table III
The Percentage of American Movies Among Films Being Shown in Various Countries

France	50%	Thailand	90%
Britain	60%	Ireland	90%
Italy	70%	Japan	31%

Movies are imported from other countries than the United States, but we shall deal only with American movies.

The content analysis of American movies has been well performed by American sociologists and social phychologists; however, what we shall discuss here is the *content of those American movies shown in Japan.* Since the war several hundred American movies have been imported into Japan and they have contributed much to the democratization of the Japanese people. The American movies shown in Japan in the one or two years immediately after the war were excellent. But the content of American movies shown in Japan in later years changed.

Table IV is a classification of 75 American movies shown in Tokyo during a two week period.

Table IV
American Movies Shown in Japan (June 1951)

	Number	Percentage	
War movies	27	37 ⎫	63%
Western movies	19	25 ⎭	
Others	29	37	
	75	100	

Over half of the "others" were melodramas.

129

Note especially that 37.3% of American films shown in Tokyo in the two weeks were war movies. This trend began in the autumn of 1950, four months after the Korean war began, with a movie entitled *The Battlefield.* Subsequently, even war movies twelve years old were imported and shown.*

The Western movies, which were 25% of the total are, of course, different from war movies, but their major themes are also gun play and killing. Over 60% of American movies in the Japanese market are sensationally aggressive films.

II. MOVIE ADVERTISING AND MOVIE JOURNALISM

The tone of advertisements is illustrated by the fact that the movie "Mata au hi made" (Until We Meet Again), an artistic, democratic film, was advertised as "The first Japanese 'kiss movie'." The advertisement for the Italian film "Open City," says "Sensation of Guns and Love."

There are now numerous movie magazines in Japan. The content of the four leading ones with the largest circulation is indicated in Table V.

Table V
An Analysis of Four Leading Movie Magazines (May 1951)

Magazine	Advertise- ments	Indirect Advertising	About Movie Stars	Technical Criticism	Other
A	0.5%	31%	54%	0 %	14.5%
B	0.5%	24%	66%	0.2%	9.3%
C	0.3%	54%	31%	0.3%	14.4%
D	0.5%	59%	28%	0.4%	12.2%
Average	0.45	42	44.7	0.22	12.7

In this table, "indirect advertising" covers such items as movie synopses, or "Introduction to New Movies," which arouses the interest of the readers in seeing particular

---

* These statements were made in 1951. H.K.

films. We shall see later that movie critics turn out to be the strongest influence in making people decide to see particular movies. The category "About movie stars" covers those articles and pictures which deal with private life of and gossip about individual stars.

III. THE MOVIE AUDIENCE

A. *Social Characteristics of the Audience:*

The social characteristics of downtown Tokyo audiences are shown in Tables VI to IX. Their range is mostly from sixteen to thirty-five, their occupations most often student or white collar, and their monthly income between 3000 and 10,000 Yen.*

This survey was made in first-run movie theaters in Tokyo. Quite different characteristics would be found if the audiences of other kinds of theaters in other districts were investigated.

Table VI
Age Distribution of the Audience:
Tokyo First-Run Theaters

Age	Male (%)	Female (%)	Total (%)
11-15	0.6	2.5	3.1
16-20	10.8	17.0	27.8
21-25	24.0	9.7	31.7
26-30	9.7	3.8	13.5
31-35	6.1	2.6	8.7
36-40	2.6	1.1	3.7
41-45	1.3	0.4	1.7
46-50	2.3	0.0	2.3
51-	0.2	0.0	0.2
Not specified	2.0	3.9	5.9
Total	59.2	40.8	100.0

* 360 Yen, according to official exchange rate, is the equivalent of 1 dollar. Thus 3000 to 10,000 Yen is $8.33 to $27.77. The average cash income of regularly employed workers in 1950 was about 9700 Yen but included in that figure are cost of living and other supplements to the basic wage which in Japan then came to about 40% of cash income. *Japan Statistical Yearbook,* 1954.

Table VII
Educational Distribution of the Audience:
Tokyo First-Run Theaters

Education	Male (%)	Female (%)	Total (%)
Primary School grad.	0.9	0.3	1.2
Middle School grad.	10.2	9.6	19.8
High School grad.	9.6	4.5	14.1
College grad.	16.7	0.5	17.2
Still in middle school	0.1	2.1	2.2
Still in high school	2.7	7.0	9.7
Still in College	17.9	7.9	25.8
Not specified	1.1	8.9	10.0
Total	59.2	40.8	100.0

Table VIII
Occupational Distribution of the Audience:
Tokyo First-Run Theaters

Occupation	Male (%)	Female (%)	Total (%)
Student	20.7	17.0	37.7
White collar	23.1	5.8	28.9
Professional	5.0	1.7	6.7
Commerce	2.4	0.2	2.6
Industry	0.6	0.0	0.6
Worker	2.4	0.0	2.4
None	2.5	10.4	12.9
Not specified	2.5	5.7	8.2
Total	59.2	40.8	100.0

Table IX
Income Distribution (omitting students)
Tokyo First Run Theater Audiences:

Monthly income	Male (%)	Female (%)	Total (%)
Lower than 3000 Yen	1.7	1.1	2.8
3000-6000	10.2	6.6	16.8
6000-9000	12.8	3.1	15.9
9000-12000	13.7	3.7	17.4
More than 12000	13.3	0.0	13.3
Not specified	3.5	30.3	33.8
Total	55.2	44.8	100.0

(Tables VI to IX are the rsult of a survey conducted June and December 1950, Tokyo.)

B. *Influences on movie selection:*

Several factors influenced audience decision to see specific films. Forty-five per cent of the audience decide to see a movie "after reading criticism" in a newspaper or magazine. The next most common influence was reading newspaper advertisements, followed by "invited by others", and "reading the original story."

C. *The frequency of movie attendance*

Attendance statistics show a Japanese movie audience of 720,000,000 annually. (Research Department, Toho Movie Production, 1949.) Surveys indicate that attendants at foreign films are more regular fans than attendants at Japanese films. The latter answered that they see movies once or twice a month, while the former said that they go three or four times a month.

Only 20% of the audience came to the theater alone and 90% of those who came alone were men.

IV. THE EFFECTS OF MOVIES

In this section we would like to consider the effects of movies upon their audiences. We shall take as examples two films produced for political propaganda.

Example A: *"Though Japan was Defeated" (June 1949)*

Originally this film was intended for showing to primary and middle school students on the recommendation of the Education Committee, but the plan was cancelled because the film had the reverse effect from that expected. Its contents were as follows:

Themes:

1) The strength of the United States, the misery of defeated Japan.

2) Soviet Union as militaristic nation.

3) The reconstruction of Japan with the support of the United States.

An effect survey was made on 500 primary and middle school pupils in Tokyo after they were shown the film. The results were as follows:

(1) Question: "How did you feel about the Kamikaze pilots?" Most of them felt they were "brave", "delightful", "great", or "real Japanese." Respect and sympathy for the Japanese army was strongly observed.

(2) Question: "What did you think of the bombing of Tokyo?" "Mortifying," "sad," "I hate the enemy," "thankful to Japanese soldiers."

(3) Question: "What did you think of General Tojo?" "Real Japanese," "sad," "he did well."

(4) Question: "Tell me why Japan lost the war?" "Poor science," "lack of bombs and food." Most of them answered in terms of the quantity of materials.

(5) Question: "What do you think of the Soviet Union?" All of them thought of it as evil, saying, "I hate it," "mean," "bad nation," or "greedy."

(6) Question: "Your comment on peace?" Their will for world peace is very strong. "Absolutely no more war," "Let's make a peaceful nation."

The result indicates that the intention of the communicator failed. With school and family education in postwar Japan not yet democratized the communicatees showed the unitended responses noted in questions 1-4.

Example B: "Four Freedoms"

Another movie, called "Four Freedoms" produced for the same purpose was shown in February 1950.
Themes of the film:
1) American democracy crushing fascism in Europe;
2) Soviet Union as new fascism;
3) Justification of righteous war, and the establishment of peace by American military strength.

Three hundred high school students in Tokyo who saw this film were interviewed. 42% of them had either lost their home by bombing or had come back from former

Japanese colonies or occupation areas, and their age was around 17 to 18. The following is the brief summary of the results of interviewing.

(1) Question: "What do you think of the Nazi army?" 60% of them praised it saying, "Brave," "magnificent," "beautiful," or "I admire it."

(2) Question: "How did you feel about the bombing of London?" Most of them answered "terrible." But some of them and not a few, said, "Do not forget revenge," or "American planes did the same thing to us."

(3) Question: "What is your opinion of the Soviet Union?" 55% of them answered that she is "arrogant," "cowardly," or "cold," and the rest also showed negative responses.

(4) Question: "Do you think that World War III will take place? Also give me the reason." 57% of them answered "yes", while 14% said "no" and 29% "don't know." The reasons for expecting war were: "As long as two incompatible ideologies exist, a war is inevitable," or "Because the atomic bomb was invented." No reasons were offered to support a negative answer.

(5) Question: "Do you think that a 'righteous' war is permissible?" 42% answered "yes," and the reasons they mentioned were: "For self-defense" or "In order to make peace." Negative answers were given by 35% saying, "It will bring misery to human beings," or "We must try to solve the problem by talking, not by violence."

Many of the results were quite similar to those in the survey about "Though Japan was Defeated." In this further case, however, special attention should be paid to the fact that respondents expected a third world war.

In these examples, the intention of the communicator was very clear and simple so that an analysis of the content and effect are far easier than for ordinary dramatic films. The intention of the communicator who attempted to give a specific idea to the communicatees failed to influence even middle school boys. The interpretation of communication effects is complex, for it involves not only rational reasoning but also the unique psychology of a people.

The following are the movies which attracted large audiences and got high repute during the first six months of 1950. (The figure in the brackets is an index number based on the average sale of a film as 100.)

1. Listen to the Voice from the Pacific*   (300)
2. Sazame Yuki**   (280)
3. Duel at Nansenzaki   (249)
4. Ginza Sanshiro   (211)

These figures, of course, reflect not solely the preference of the audience, for many other factors too affect the popularity of a film. However, some index of the political direction of popular taste is the fact that "Listen to the Voice from the Pacific" was the most popular film, and also that "The Town of Violence"*** had an index number of 141.

---

* A movie based on the book of the same title. It is an anthology of letteds and diaries of student-soldiers who died in the war, always doubtful about the purpose of the war. In effect, this movie, as well as the book, was anti-militaristic and anti-war.

** This title has been translated as *The Makibka Sisters* for its American publication, but it is "an almost untranslatable expression that refers to snow falling in very fine flakes." (E. Schneider, "Modern Japanese Literature," *The Atlantic,* Jan., 1955, p. 168.) The movie is based on a book written by Junichiro Tanizaki, one of the leading Japanese authors.

*** "The Town of Violence," a movie based on a factual story, was made by a group of socially conscientious artists. It is the people of the community, fought against gangsters who had infiltrated the town in cooperation with a corrupt mayor and officers. The location of the filming was in the town itself despite interference.

THE JAPANESE SPIRIT AS IT APPEARS IN MOVIES*

by Taihei Imamura

Japanese conversation is tedious. The Japanese achieves his purpose in a roundabout way. People start conversing on such topics as weather and gossip. It is in the last part of the conversation that they come to the major subject. Consequently, one often cannot discern the intention of the speaker. In meetings, too, the main subject often comes at the end, and most of the time is occupied by chatter. One often finds that little time remains to discuss the major topic for which the meeting was called. Then the participants try hurriedly to reach a conclusion. The conclusion is reached not after careful discussion, but in order to finish within the limited time remaining. In such instances, intuition is demanded rather than careful reasoning.

In speeches or writing, too, there are usually long preliminaries to the major subject. Again, when the speaker reaches his subject, he frequently finds but a few minutes remain to him. A Japanese is likely to rely, in

---

* Published in *Science of Thought* (*Shiso no Kagaku*), Vol. 5, No. 2, 1950.

these cases, on metaphor and suggestion instead of proof. His thinking in this mode, it seems to me, is due to the fact that a Japanese accepts things as they are rather than attempting to reconstruct them mentally.

His thought is not trained to distinguish essences from phenomena, so he speaks of a phenomenon in the state of chaos, and in the process of speaking he tries to clarify the idea. That is why Japanese conversation is long and tedious. Since the speaker wants to express the phenomena he sees without analysis, inference, and judgment, there is neither definition nor abstraction. In consequence a conversation is prolonged.

The language of those such as old village women, who have no chance to develop logical reasoning, is descriptive. They try to recall concrete and specific scenes instead of engaging in abstraction. For this reason, it is difficult to grasp their essential points from the content of their conversation. They can suggest the important points by sound and gesture only. At one time the speaker may speak in a very low voice and stare at the listener in order to draw his attention. When he comes to the most important point, gesture and facial expression take the lead, and the content is merely meaningless repetition of some word, such as an exclamation or conjunction.

What we are describing is an approach in which a person thinks in the process of description and in the process of feeling. For those who do that, thinking is not distinct from intuition, nor is a phenomenon distinct from its essence. Thinking flows along with the stream of phenomena. An object is not analytically reconstructed by thinking but is described as it appears. The essence is never explored. The nature of a problem can only be suggested by concrete description. Repetition of a description of detailed tedious description can at best suggest the nature of an important problem.

However, it is impossible to continue description endlessly. A Japanese tries to solve that problem by suddenly changing the topic and the situation. This method is both escape and aggression. There is a proverb in Japan which says: "When in haste, take a roundabout way." Japanese thinking is the application of this proverb. A Japanese thinks while he is in escape from the subject. He escapes in order to approach the subject again. While he is far from the subject, he thinks about how to explain the point and what conclusion he should reach. When he finds a cue for returning to the topic, he goes back to the original subject again with his new ideas.

A man who goes to ask a favor begins conversation with unconcerned remarks on the weather and with miscellaneous gossip. The listener, however busy he is, and even when he knows the visitor's intention, pays serious attention to these diversionary topics. The more important the subject, the more the idle talk is prolonged. After this meaningless talk, the speaker suddenly approaches the subject, saying, "By the way, frankly..." If the listener does not respond to the approach, the speaker changes the topic again, and with carefully calculated timing, comes back to the subject again, saying, "Now, as to the problem I was going to discuss..." In Japan, a person who is skillful in changing the topic and situation in this way is called "mature" and "smart". It is not logic but tact which operates in these cases—a tact which induces the listener to identify with the speaker. The speaker is not asking comprehension from the listener.

The Japanese, being neither analytical nor inductive, does his thinking during the process of speaking. A plan is made as one goes along, not before. When the plan is found to be unsuccessful, the speaker prolongs the talk and awaits the listener's identification with him. In other words, there is a ceaseless prolongation awaiting a fortuitous cue.

Writing follows the same method employed in daily conversation. The Japanese writes a treatise like an essay. What he wants to say becomes clear to him only while he is writing or speaking. Most people write without careful preparation, expecting that something will emerge in the process. However, in the process of writing, ideas are apt to turn in unexpected directions. Thus topics change frequently.

The changes in topic do not serve to clarify the nature of the problem. They represent only a shift in the aspect of the problem which is observed. There is thus a quantitative accumulation of aspects. And with the increase in number of aspects, the author expects to reach a clear idea of the nature of the problem. This approach characterizes writers, as well as old village women. The Japanese attitude is phenomenological, and as such is indefinite. Phenomena are accepted as wholes, without analysis or definition.

The mental attitude above described is well represented in the grammatical structure of Japanese, in which the verb comes last and the subject is not easily defined. While Europeans define the subject first, the Japanese leave the subject ambiguous in relation to its predicate. The verb, as Mr. Okubo has pointed out, comes at the end, as in "Hito ga Inu o Utsu" *(A man a dog beats)*, while in English the verb appears before the object: "A man beats a dog." The construction of English is active and positive toward phenomena; Japanese, on the other hand, is passive and negative. It expresses an attitude which attempts to avoid the clear definition of a phenomenon.

The tendency toward indefiniteness can be also seen in the usage of words. The fact that Japanese grammar lacks article, number, and gender, is a kind of indefiniteness. "Hito" (man) in Japanese can mean "man in general" ("a man") or "a particular man" ("the man".) Since there is no distinction between the plural and singular form of nouns it can also mean "men" or "the men." This indefiniteness gives Japanese the attribute of suggestiveness. In English, "a dog" or "a man" is itself an element of a sentence, but in Japanese every noun must be combined with an auxiliary suffix (Joshi); a noun becomes a sentence element only when an auxiliary suffix has been added. As Mr. Izuru Shinmura said, in Japanese the meaning of a sentence does not change if the word order is changed. It changes in meaning only when the auxiliary suffix is replaced. This makes Japanese a more suggestive and more complicated language.

Some Japanese words, as Mr. Nyozekan Hasegawa points out, have two opposite meanings. For example, "ee" means "yes" (and also "good"). But when this word is pronounced long and strongly, it means an absolute "no". "Un", which means "yes" also means "no" when pronounced as "U-un."* The same sound has two absolutely opposite meanings, depending on the speaker's intonation and physical expression. The interjection "Ho" sometimes connotes contempt. When one says, "He is clever," he may really mean "He is cunning." "You are great" sometimes means "You are a fool." More than in most languages the meaning of a Japanese word varies depending on the speaker's intonation and gesture. That fact evidences the absence of clear definition of words, and also that language is being used descriptively, emotionally, and dramatically.

Such characteristics of language can be regarded as the propensity to receive a phenomenon as it appears and not to codify it. A Japanese describes a phenomenon emotionally and does not think about its essence. He tries to reach the essence by intuition in the process of description. It is the method of the alchemist who awaits chance success from a plethora of effort. One can easily note this characteristic in our meetings, conversations, and writings.

The Japanese character, as revealed in Japanese movies, shares these attitudes. Most Japanese movies, for example, lack structure, a characteristic they share with the poor

---

* It is as in the case of the English expression uh-huh (yes) and uh-uh (no). Ed.

modern drama in Japan and with many Japanese novels. The more artistic Japanese movies are those of the genre of self-novel,* or essay and personal diary. In these, the observer in characteristic Japanese fashion, endeavors to recall a phenomenon instead of analytically reconstructing it. The best examples are the movies directed by Yasujiro Ozu. His recent work, "A Hen in the Wind," like his earlier productions, "Tokyo Inn," "The Only Son," and "Father and Son" is weak in dramatic construction. In these movies, the casts are very small and the stories are monotonous and without climax.

A drop of water falls to the calm surface of a pond, and starts a water ring—after that deep silence again. Mr. Ozu's movies are represented in this scene. He describes the environment surrounding man rather than his psychology and personality. Furthermore, the environment thus described is natural and scenic rather than social. Mr. Ozu's description of an environment not necessarily related to the theme of the movie but has its own significance apart from the plot. The gas tank and the bank of the Sumida River, which repeatedly appeared in "A Hen in the Wind," are examples. The audience remember pictorial scenes like a school ground with an elm tree, the road where drug-sellers pass, a sooty oil lamp hanging from the ceiling, or a field at the edge of town where a gas tank is seen, even after they forget the story of the movie, for the scenes have priority over drama and are loved apart from the drama.

In the love of natural scenery we can find the negative and passive attitudes of the Japanese. It is an escape from society into nature, and from character descriptions of events and people into descriptions of natural scenes.

---

* Shi-shosetsu (self-novel) is the dominant genre in Japanese literature. Most of the leading authors write about their own daily experience in the first person. These self-novels are usually very short stories. It has been argued by the literary critic, S. Ito, that the authors tend to describe only their own personal affairs, because novelists in Japanese society, having become over-westernized, are not able to maintain touch with the common man's life.

If the conflict in the drama is the reflection of social contradictions, the attitude which I am discussing is one which refuses to clarify the contradictions, i.e., the nature of an object. So Mr. Ozu's descriptions of the environment are always static and on the fence. In his movies society is observed indirectly through nature. Capitalist society is portrayed by such scenes as a gas tank on an uncultivated field, a small junk on a dirty canal, or a baby's diaper drying in a back alley. Society is seen only from a distance, as a natural scene, and people are but accessories. Natural scenes are shown unconnected with the characters or the drama. Like paintings, they are impressive, but never become a part of drama.

Not only is this true of Mr. Ozu's movies; it is characteristic of Japanese films. The scenes portrayed in them do not elucidate a man's behavior and its necessity. Nature, as portrayed in them is mostly seasonal nature, which has no relation to man's psychology and personality. The films express the Japanese admiration of and attachment to nature which were formed through traditional Japanese poetry, the Waka and the Haiku. We can mention as remarkable examples "The Soil" directed by Mr. Tomu Uchida, and "The Horse" by Mr. Kajiro Yamamoto. These describe mostly seasonal changes in villages, not the problems of rural society. This is the very approach which such feudal artists as Okyo and Eitoku employed in their painting of the four seasons in nature. The contemporary Japanese film shares the basic attitude toward reality of the traditional arts.

This lyrical approach is found among the most intelligent directors, such as Yasujiro Ozu or Fumio Kamei. Love of nature and lyricism have been basic characteristics of Japanese movies. They have not tried to analyze man and human relations nor to clarify the nature of society, but rather to symbolize society through nature and to see society from a distance. The lack of drama in Japanese films is the result. The natural scene in the movie is not an element of the drama, but an element which opposes the drama.

In Mr. Ozu's work, the natural scene does not contribute to the development of the plot; it stops it. The gas tank in "A Hen in the Wind" is like a refrain in a lyric poem with no connection to the development of the drama. When the director looks at the natural scene, his observation is independent of the dramatic construction—in a word, the drama is stopped for a while. These scenes sometimes resemble impressionist paintings, but they are not naturalistic in a strict sense. They continue to be connected with the themes of "snow, moon, and flowers" which were characteristic of the feudal arts. The mood of feudal artists, who escaped the oppression of lords by attending to the moon and the beauty of flowers, is still alive in Japanese movies. Thus the basic quality of the movies is supported by a traditional temper called sympathetic sadness.*

Many historical movies, for example, describe the wandering of Ronin** and Yakuza***, pursued by officers. The natural scenes surrounding them are seen through sad eyes. The lyric natural scene in a Japanese movie is always an expression of sorrowfulness.

Examples of such scenes are:

Broken kite on the top of a withered tree. Clouds pass by quickly. ("Daibosatsu Toge")
A Yakuza was killed. The bell of a temple is heard ringing far away. ("Gambler of the Town")
Kunisada Chuji runs away along a road in the midst of a rice field. Scattered pine trees, white road, his shadow, and a frog croaking. ("Kunisada Chuji")

---

* Mono-no Aware—The translation of the term was suggested by Miss Tamako Niwa at Harvard Yenching Institute. However, the implication is very complicated. The term includes the following attributes: "sadness," "uncertainty of life and things," "beauty," "calmness." This term expresses a traditional Japanese art concept, influenced largely by Buddhism. "Sad beauty" as used by American literary critics may share some elements with this term. Typical of this stream of thought are the poets Basho and Saigyo.
** Ronin: a masterless Samurai.
*** Yakuza: see the "Analysis of Yakuza Fiction" in this volume.

Street outside the town. Unemployed father and his son going away. ("Tokyo Inn")
A man, infected with tuberculosis, looks at a dirty marsh. An old doll floats on the surface. ("Drunken Angel")

These natural scenes express the philosophy of uncertainty, pitifulness, and instability of man's life, which Saigyo expressed in his poems and Basho in his Haiku. It involves neither struggle for life nor willingness to overcome its sadness. It is the attitude of a Buddhist priest who looks upon the human world from a distance. This way of thinking remains attractive to the Japanese, insofar as the social oppression which produced this attitude continues to exist. Japanese film artists, like their ancestors, remain unconcerned spectators. They assume that to be a spectator—to see society from outside—is to be objective. So they express their most impressive and conclusive points by the description of nature. The natural scenes in Japanese movies are therefore symbolic, as in Japanese paintings and poetry. They are symbolic because nature is independent of the drama. Examples of this symbolism are a crow cawing at the burned-down house in "The Clan of Abe" (directed by Hisatora Kumagai), or a time-withered tree in a wild field in "Nightingale" (directed by Mr. Shiro Toyoda). These have the same indefiniteness that is expressed by Japanese black ink painting. The Japanese mentality was trained by escaping from society and contemplating nature. This mentality is static and negative.

The reason the Japanese admires natural scenes is that he wants to escape from society. The poor dramatic construction of Japanese movies is the expression of the weakness of Japanese reasoning. The fact that Japanese movies lack tempo and speed indicates the ineffectiveness of Japanese social action. Japanese films do not analyze personalities and their relationships with others. They do not try to grasp the essential contradictions among men. The drama lacks motive for development, and characters, therefore, do not change. In the film world there is neither contradiction nor opposition; all is calm and peaceful. Mr. Ozu's plots are mere changes of composition, like pictures in a photograph album. There is no dynamism. There is no indication of the development of life. There is merely an accumulation of pictures. The film is a picture scroll.

Here we find again the technique of description which we found in Japanese daily conversation. Ordinary conversation we noted, merely describes a phenomenon, instead of cause and effect relationships. It deals with an event without the "why" of the event.

Thus, the style of movies resembles that of a sketch, essay, or personal diary. In fact, often they are based on children's compositions, children's stories, and diaries, besides self-novels. The semi-documentary quality of Japanese films is not the conscious application of documentary film technique. It is an avoidance of dramatic construction and an escape to nature.

It is natural, therefore, that in spite of the new possibilities which motion picture technology has brought, the ideal of the Japanese film approaches the style and technique of a self-novel. Ozu's "Tokyo Inn" was suggested by the novel "Manazuru" by Naoya Shiga, one of Japan's leading novelists. Such directors as Sadao Yamanaka and Mansaku Itami have introduced a new approach into historical movies by the application of self-novel technique. They describe historic heroes in terms of human interest —a loyal feudal Samurai is described as an individual suffering from a digestive disease because he over-indulged in sweets. The significance of these movies is that the heroic characters of feudal stories are reduced to the status of common men. That is the approach of Naoya Shiga. It is the technique of the self-novel.

The narrative character of Japanese art is another expression of the Japanese acceptance of things as they appear. Japanese drama has always been combined with narrative, e.g., Utai or Joruri (story-telling accompanied by simple string instruments). The picture scroll, in which a story is developed through a sequence of pictures, is a common form of traditional painting. Traditional story-telling still exists and the film story is a modification of this narrative mode.

The popularity of story-telling indicates that the people have little interest in the analysis of human psychology and character and are interested rather in the action of the story itself. This is, I repeat, the attitude which does not try to analyze and reconstruct a phenomenon. Since the event is described phenomenally, the description necessarily becomes tedious. But Japanese art has a technique to handle the tediousness; that is the simplification of the description.

Japanese art develops through increasing simplification. In Haiku* poetry everything that can be, is omitted; what remains is an irreducible simplification. The black-ink painting of mountains and streams is also an art of simplification. Birds, trees, rocks, are described in simple brush strokes of black ink. Other examples are the pantomime of No and Kabuki plays, which are performed before a colorless screen.

At the end of this simplication, the Japanese finds his conclusion. It is not a conclusion reached after observation and analysis, but a conclusion which intuition reaches through simplification. The Japanese finds the nature of a problem when everything which can be excluded is excluded. What results is rather a symbol than a description. It is rather a suggestion than an explicit demonstration. The reason that short stories have been dominant among

---

* Haiku. This form of poetry was very neatly summarized by Earl Roy Miner: "The Haiku, which was developed in the 17th Century, is composed of 17 syllables. Haiku is a poetry of nature in the Buddho-Taoist conception which includes man as an integral part *within* nature. It is based largely on natural images with religious overtones, and each Haiku is traditionally required to have one 'season-word' or expression which implies a time of year." "Forms of Japanese Poetry," *The Atlantic Monthly,* January 1955, p. 166.

Japanese naturalistic writers lies also in this pattern of simplification. Long, detailed Japanese novels are tedious and monotonous, so a well simplified short story is more highly regarded than a large-scale work. This explains much of the reputation of a writer of short stories like Naoya Shiga whose descriptions of scenes are highly symbolic.

Japanese films also have this tendency toward simplicity. The most artistic movies, as opposed to long and tedious melodramas, are composed by simplification. The movies directed by Ozu, Yamanaka, and Itami, are concise and neat. The artistic value of a Japanese movie comes out only when it has been simplified like Haiku poetry. The montage theory of the Soviet Union has influenced Japanese movie technique. However, the montage in Japanese movies is used as are the Haiku descriptions of nature, so that it is not intellectual, ideological, or dramatic. If becomes an extension of the simplification technique of the traditional arts.

For instance, the heroine's new hope for her life is symbolized by the rising sun behind a factory and the sound of a siren heard in the morning fog ("The Life of a Woman" by Fumio Kamei). The suffering of life is suggested by a sooty oil-lamp, and hope is symbolized by the morning school ground where boys are in gymnastics class ("The Only Son" by Ozu). There again we find the delicate transfer of the motif to the metaphor of the natural scene, as in traditional poetry.

The series of documentary films directed by Fumio kamei ("Shanghai," "Nanking," and "Kobayashi Issa") is representative in this connection, and we can regard them as the most magnificent reconstruction of Haiku which describe human affairs only through the description of natural scenes.

A butterfly flies over a wash-basin thrown out on the battlefield. ("Shanghai")

148

A butterfly around the shoulder of a tired soldier, a bright flower at his worn-out shoes. ("Nanking")
An old farmer bowing at a big tree. His house is burning behind him. ("Fighting Soldiers")
The body of a dead soldier is being burned. It is cloudy and smoky. The voice of the priest is reading the Buddhist scripture. ("Nanking")
An old farmer is taking an outdoor bath. A mountain with snow is seen far away. A nightingale sings on a plum tree. ("Kobayashi Issa")

They are beautiful montages of images and sounds, and at the same time inherit the style of Haiku description. The misery of war is symbolized by butterflies and flowers, and the poverty of a Japanese village is indicated by frosted fields and an old warehouse. Society is thus observed only through nature, and the director's thinking about society is symbolically simplified by natural scenes. The course of Japanese thinking progresses through the changes in these natural scenes. At the critical climax of a story, the Japanese movie escapes into nature. In "Daibosatsu Toge" by Hiroshi Inagaki, there is a scene in which two Samurai are about to fight with swords before their lord. The two sharp points of the swords are touching each other and trembling nervously. The spectators are watching anxiously. At this tense climax, the director shifts the camera. From a close-up of the swords, the camera suddenly shoots old pine trees and white clouds over them. It is a conversion from tension to the opposite. It is an escape from the dynamic to the static. The Japanese intensifies the expression by the conversion and escape. It is a positive use of negativism. The death of a Yakuza is symbolized by the sound of a temple bell. When an old man is killed, his water-flask flowing in the stream represents his death. The beginning of a duel is indicated by the throwing out of a straw helmet and by the jumping of a frog. The water ring which the frog makes symbolizes a man's death. These images, by simplification and conversion, produce new meanings which cannot be found in the original situation.

Eisenstein showed that the opposition of two images

produces a new meaning. Haiku has used this technique in Japanese art. However, the important point is that the montage in Haiku poetry is always emotional and the quality of the emotion is always essentially the same. It is the idea of indefiniteness of time and space and that man and his life are small and uncertain. This is a Buddhist conception. The montage in Japanese movies is a contemporary adaption of the feeling of uncertainty in Buddhism. The symbols employed in the movie are exactly those of Haiku, which merely suggest infinite time and space. The clouds, the flowing stream, and the sound of the temple bell, these are the symbols of the uncertainty of human life. Behind this there is a Buddhist doctrine— the belief in the absolute and infinite value. That doctrine regards life as a temporary resting place, man as power- less; it purports to solve that problem by his being a spectator.

New developments in Japanese movies will be possible when this traditional idea is rejected, when Japanese movie makers actively describe society instead of nature. But such change in Japanese motion pictures implies changes in Japanese ways of thinking.

AN ANALYSIS OF
KIMI NO NA WA
(WHAT IS YOUR NAME?)
A SERIAL RADIO DRAMA*

by Tsutomo Ono

THE STORY**

One night in 1945, during an American air raid, a girl named Machiko was helped by an unknown young man on Sukiya Bridge, Tokyo. The man asked her, "What is your name?" but she only answered, "If we both survive, let us meet at this spot on the same day in six months' time."

The six months passed, and the young man, Haruki, awaited her on the bridge. She came. But Machiko, who had lost her parents, had meanwhile been persuaded by her uncle to a marriage with Katsunori Hamaguchi, a young governmental official. It was the day before the wedding when she met Haruki again.

Within three years of this reunion, Katsunori had become chief of the public relations section of a bureau, and coincidentally Haruki had been working in the same

* This paper was originally published in *Shiso no Kagaku*, Vol. 1, No. 6, October 1954.
** "Kimi No Na Wa" was first broadcast on N.H.K., then published as a book, and at the same time produced as a movie. It has been estimated that at least ten million people (one-eighth of the Japanese

section as chief editor of a public relations magazine. The new section chief, Katsunori, invited Haruki to his house, knowing that Machiko and Haruki had earlier been in love. He wished them to forswear their love before him. Machiko was sorrowful at her husband's suspicion, but at last she told Haruki, before her husband, that she would never see him again. And for her sake, Haruki also swore.

A few days later, Haruki's sister was mistaken for a prostitute and arrested. Katsunori found out about this scandal and forced Haruki to resign.

Machiko, much ashamed of her husand's underhand behavior, visited Haruki's boarding house to apologize, but Haruki would not see her because of the promise. Her husband's mother, Tokue, was angry when she learned that Machiko had visited Haruki. She called Machiko a faithless woman.

Insulted and scolded by Tokue, Machiko fled to her uncle's house on Sado Island, a few hundred miles from Tokyo, and tried to kill herself by jumping from a mountain bridge. Haruki, who had followed, appeared suddenly and saved her. Taking her into his arms, he said, "Let us live somewhere together!" But Machiko answered sadly, "I am soon to have a baby."

Machiko returned to her husband's family and had a miscarriage. Tokue again complained, saying that the miscarriage was intentional. She thought the baby was Haruki's.

Meanwhile Haruki had gone to Hokkaido, where a classmate managed a ranch, to forget about Machiko. He decided to live on the farm permanently.

On the farm there was a lovely girl of mixed Japanese and Ainu* blood, Yumi, who fell in love with Haruki.

---

population) saw the movie. The stole which Machiko wore in the movie became a nation-wide fashion and many things in the drama were imitated by young people. So an analysis of the story is important to students of communication problems.
* The Ainu are remnants of the original inhabitants of Japan, much like the American Indians.

In Tokyo, Machiko, unable to stop the insults of her mother-in-law, at last called upon her aunt from Sado to negotiate a divorce. Katsunori agreed to a separation, but refused a divorce.

Machiko went to Hokkaido to seek Haruki, and there found Yumi, the other girl. One day, Haruki took Machiko in his carriage to Mashu Lake, a beautiful sight-seeing spot. Yumi, jealous, follows them on horseback. And Samuro, Yumi's fiancée, a young Ainu boy, chased Yumi, also on horseback. Yumi by accident fell off the cliff into the lake, and Samuro, who followed her, died. Yumi, who was only injured, told Machiko, "Haruki is yours."

A letter arrived from the Tokyo District Court addressed to both Machiko and Haruki, saying that Katsunori had brought charges against them. Machiko went back to Tokyo to settle the matter.

Katsunori offered to withdraw the charges on condition that Machiko go to Kyushu, two thousand miles from Hokkaido. She accepted the condition and went to work in a hotel in the Unzen National Park.

Haruki came back to Tokyo and found a job as editor of the *Women's Review*. One day Katsunori visited Haruki in his office and said, "If Machiko will marry a man other than you, I will divorce her." But later Katsunori himself became desirous of a divorce because he found a profitable new bride, the daughter of a high government official. He signed an unconditional statement of divorcement.

Haruki, a journalist, was then appointed as a correspondent in Europe. Before his departure, he visited Machiko at Unzen. Machiko said, "I will wait for your return."

Two or three months later Haruki received a telegram from Japan saying, "Machiko in critical condition." He flew back to Japan and visited Machiko in a hospital. Seeing Haruki, Machiko recovered and a new hopeful world was theirs.

ANALYSIS

The city of Kiriu in Gunma prefecture is a city of textile workers, and my wife is one of them. Last fall she told me that the working girls, though very busy on the fall shipments and even working overtime until 10 p.m., stopped their machines every Thursday at 8.30 p.m. to listen to the radio together. Their wages are paid on a piecework basis, so that thirty minutes of work means something to them. But the "Kimi No Na Wa" program was much more attractive than the few tens of yen payment which they might get, Since I knew the poverty of these workers, I was surprised at the attraction of the radio drama.

Meanwhile, in another factory, the girls started work at 4 a.m. on Thursdays in order to be able to listen to their radios at home in the evening. Moreover, when the movie, "Kimi No Na Wa" came to the city, the girls took a taxi from work to the movie theater. (For these girls a taxi could mean two or three days' wages.) These strange things have happened.

These girl workers are generally considered vulgar and poorly educated; they use boys' language, and their main topic of conversation is men. Whenever they have extra money, they buy candy with it. However, in a city like Kiriu, it is their labor that supports the local industry. In such a milieu, literature or culture which does not appeal to these girls is rather meaningless. It is necessary for intellectuals to comprehend "Kimi No Na Wa" rather than to criticize it ideologically from the outside.

What is it that led girl weavers of sixteen or seventeen to go to the movie by taxi? What drove them to weave from 4 a.m. in December in an unheated factory? That seemed important to me. I wanted to learn from various people what impressions or opinions they had of "Kimi No Na Wa." Not only young girls but also old women were deeply interested in the story, especially in the relationship between the heroine and her mother-in-law. Most men, on the other hand, showed no interest. Men, both intellectuals and workers whom I met, said, "Nonsense." But men who heard the radio with their wives said, "It is not so bad." The more I heard, the more interested I became in obtaining a clear understanding by some systematic method.

INVESTIGATION AND RESULT

I found it difficult to construct a questionnaire and select its items. Abstract questions would not be easy for women to answer, especially for women with little education. On the other hand, detailedly structured questions might not elicit the subjects' unique responses. So I decided to ask first which plots they liked and disliked, and second their evaluations of the hero and the heroine.

Table I shows who the respondents were and how they had been exposed to "Kimi No Na Wa." Of course, the numbers are very small and it is not possible to draw wide conclusions from these data. But we do find that all the married women knew "Kimi No Na Wa" by radio, though half of them had not seen the movie; unmarried women were familiar with "Kimi No Na Wa" both by radio and movie.

Table II shows how this drama was received by the women. There was much difference between the reception of the radio and movie version. The radio version was liked, but the movie was not well received. If we put the distribution of evaluations into two categories, namely "plus" ("good," "very good") and "minus" ("poor," "bad"), then for the radio the ratio between "plus" and "minus" is 21:4 while for the movie, it is 7:12.

"Machiko stole," "Machiko rock" and "Haruki pants" are contemporary commodity brand names taken from the film. Keiko Kishi (who played Machiko) and Keiji Sada (who played Haruki) won much fame. Yet people criticized the movie severely. The film version was a more typically commercial love story.

None of those who heard "Kimi No Na Wa" on the radio expressed a negative response. Yet more strongly positive attitudes were found more often among married than among unmarried women. The content of "Kimi No Na Wa" is more closely attuned to the mentality of married women, for it deals with traditionalism and with the power-lessness of women in the family system.

Generally it is said that "Kimi No Na Wa" is the love story of Machiko and Haruki, but the audience seems to have received it as a story of trouble and resistance in the traditional family.

Let us now consider the views expressed about the good and bad points in the film. The most common favor-able theme is: "I was impressed by the love of Machiko and Haruki." Their platonic love was unchanging. They continually wished each other's happiness. These are the themes that the audience considered beautiful and pure. As one woman put it, "Since there are many immoral events in present society, the story is very attractive." Though people today may have lost sexual morality and public morals and there may be much corruption, yet as seen from the responses, admiration for beauty and purity still remains. People yearn for them. They wish to devote them selves to their lovers and to themselves have such a beautiful love, though the wish is unrealizable. This unrealistic wish, deeply hidden in their hearts, was fulfilled in the story, and that is why they were attracted.

Another reason given by the girls for liking the story is that "it might happen to anyone." "The dispute between the heroine and her mother-in-law is a very common thing at present," and "in the latter part, the bride made her mother-in-law tender." In short, the girls are attracted because the author describes a quarrel which happens often in present-day Japan and describes troubles, sorrow, struggles, and pleasures which every Japanese can under-

156

stand. The people in this story are neither extremely traditional nor extremely progressive. They are figures familiar to everyone.

One factory girl said, "All of us heard the program as if we were Machiko." People suffering from the feudalistic Japanese family system sympathized with the characters. Not only is the story familiar, but in addition the struggle against traditionalism in "Kimi No Na Wa" appealed strongly to the Japanese heart.

Let us summarize now the unfavorable opinions and the opinions of those who said they could not understand the story. One girl said, "The beginning of the story was good but in the latter part similar events happened over and over again. The radio drama ended more simply than I expected, so I was not satisfied." (An 18 year old office girl.)

"From the middle of the story things were so confused that I really couldn't understand." (A 17 year old operative.)

"I think the end is too simple." (A 28 year old housewife.)

Criticisms were that the story was too long, that similar events repeatedly took place for the sake of sensationalism, and that "the ending was too simple" because Haruki and Machiko who had suffered so much, could not achieve a happy ending so easily.

Another opinion: "The story is so idealistic that there are many points which are not realistic." (A 20 year old girl.) Though unconcerned with any theory of realism, the girl who expressed that opinion indicates that if a movie or radio drama has no realistic connection with her, she dislikes it. The story was designed to attract audience attention to each specific scene instead of by the development of the hero and heroine, but this technique did not always satisfy the women.

Other unfavorable opinions were: "Katsunori is cruel to Machiko." (A 28 year old farmer's wife.)

"Katsunori didn't understand his wife." (A 28 year old housewife.)

The respondents who said these things were identifying strongly. They took the story seriously and felt hate rather than feeling that the story was not interesting. Both of them were housewives.

Now we turn to the criticisms of the major characters in this story.

HARUKI

In general he is regarded as an ideal, but weak-willed man. Classifying the opinions about him into three categories,—favorable, unfavorable, and mixed—we find that in the case of unmarried women, unfavorable plus mixed exceed favorable by a ratio of 9:4, while among married women the figure is reversed, 5:7. (See Table III.) That may indicate a difference between the generations. Illustrative comments follow.

Unmarried, favorable:

An ideal man with deep affection and kindness." (A 24-year-old factory girl.)

Unmarried, mixed:

"Though I understand his devotion to Machiko, I wish he was more manly." (An operative.)

Unmarried, unfavorable:

"I think gentle Haruki might be a good match for Machiko but his character seems to be superficial, not realistic." (A 19 year old weaver.)

Married, favorable:

"He has sacrificed himself to save people." (A 61 year old woman.)

Married, unfavorable:

"If he loved Machiko truly, he shouldn't have been satisfied even if Machiko was happy to marry Katsunori.' (A 22 year old weaver.)

As seen from these examples, the favorable points are "his big heart," "gentleness" and "devotion," while unfavorable points are "not manly," "negative," and "not realistic."

158

MACHIKO

Most unmarried women, as seen in Table IV, were critical of Machiko and said that she lacked a strong will. Married women, on the contrary, supported her and were attracted especially by her "tender heart".

Married, mixed:

"She is so gentle that she is loved by everybody, but she depends too much upon others." (A 22 year old office girl.)

Unmarried, critical:

"A nice girl is not attracted by another man's small kindnesses when she is in love." (A 17-year old weaver.)

Married, favorable:

"I like her very much. She made her mother-in-law happy even though she suffered from her. I sympathize with her." (The 55 year old wife of a weaving shed owner.)

Married, mixed:

"She is appealing, but unrealistic." (A 52 year old woman.)

Married, critical:

"She is very conservative; not in the least progressive." (A 22 year old weaver.)

In a word, women criticized Machiko severely, although they were deeply attracted by the radio and the movie. Why? The following view may provide the answer: "To tell the truth, though I wrote only bad criticisms, I set my hope on every Thursday night and listened to the radio so intently that the movie didn't satisfy my great expectations." (18 years old.)

Even people who were absorbed and deeply moved by the story, when they are about to write a comment become more or less critical. To my surprise, young women were critical of Machiko, regardless of whether they were married or unmarried. Perhaps they had emotional sympathy with the traditional moral code even while rationally they resist it. Women's opinions about Machiko varied according to their family status and generation. Old women expected the submission of the bride; young women wished freedom.

Next we shall examine the criticisms of Tokue. Tokue is described in this story as a wicked mother-in-law, and so is criticized by most. Because "she is feudalistic and doesn't understand the young couple, I hate her." (A 44 year old woman without occupation.) But there are some who are more or less sympathetic: "she is not so wicked by nature." "Her sort is very common at present." A woman said, "I think Japanese feudalistic morals made her such a seemingly wicked woman." (A 22 year old weaver.)

Before closing the description of the results in our investigation I would like to note some general comments which appeared in the questionnaire. There were five opinions which ascribed practical usefulness to the story. "Both the young and the old should hear and see 'Kimi No Na Wa' for their daily experience." (A 61 year old woman.) "I am a mother-in-law and want to have a pleasant home, so I want to hear that sort of a drama." (A 61 year old housewife.) "It is a good teacher for our married life." (A 28 year old housewife.)

POSITIVE AND NEGATIVE ASPECTS OF "KIMI NO NA WA"

The common people of Japan, especially women, and not only the weavers, work hard these days. They have no time to appreciate literature, but they can listen to a radio story while working. However, the popularity of "Kimi No Na Wa," requires additional explanation. The audience, in my opinion, does not appreciate the drama so much for its own sake, as for an opportunity to contemplate their own problems through the story. Our problem, therefore, is not that of finding out what was in "Kimi No Na

Wa," but to learn how it was perceived by its audience. This story has a content that can be shared by Japanese women suffering under feudalism and war damage. Most women who heard the radio or saw the movie received from it more than a love story about Haruki and Machiko. They interpreted it as a story about persons denied happiness by outside pressures and weaknesses within themselves. It is a story about persons trying to marry, but beset by many troubles. Essentially, it is a story about the struggle for freedom.

The author, Mr. Kikuta, has said: "In the provinces there are many people who are still suffering under traditional thought and customs. I hope they will not have to endure an unhappy married life like Machiko's." In a sense he was successful. Having heard the radio, a weaver thought "Machiko is foolish, why doesn't she give him a decided answer?" A housewife whom I know, after hearing the radio with her mother-in-law, said, "The radio said the very thing that I have wanted to say." Perhaps many people are still troubled with problems similar to Machiko's.

Japanese women are charmed by the story of a weak and traditional woman who endures hardship and at last finds her own way out by her own decision.

Furthermore, because the drama treated private troubles with their social implications, it conveyed a progressive tone to the audience. If one reads "Kimi No Na Wa" carefully he will find social explanations of the quarrel in the story in terms of feudalism, war, bureaucracy and so on. The author treated these issues emotionally as "tragic, social intercourse between man and man."

Furthermore, he teaches that "man is neither good nor bad by nature. There is greater reason why quarrels and shadows appear in the human world. Men need reason and love to understand and help each other." All the people in the story are nice. Even Tokue who was the most wicked, is described as a traditional woman whose only wish was her son's success after her husband's death.

In addition, the author showed a rare humanism toward the poor and the weak. The beauty of "Kimi No Na Wa" came from this, and also from its sympathy with people troubled and under pressure and with those who assert their petty resistance to ugly society. Everybody loves this feature of the story for its idealistic quality of showing universal tolerance for every human being.

There is, however, a danger that the statement of the sorrowfulness of social intercourse between man and man in the human world may lead to an attitude of resignation. The negative aspect of "Kimi No Na Wa" stems directly from its fantastic and unrealistic beauty. Though the author proposed social problems, he suggests individual love and good will as their solution. Sympathetic tears, however, cannot be more than tears. This weakness was criticized by many women, as I noted in the preceding section. Though politically "Kimi No Na Wa" may be a conservative work, many people seek to satisfy progressive aspirations through its drama. These it partly fails to satisfy.

A second weakness of the story is the stress on melodramatic events instead of on scenes concerned with women's actual life. There are too many tedious events inserted for sensationalism, which do not have any connection with the development of drama. As some women said, "Similar scenes appear over and over again," and "tedious."

Table I

To What Extent Are You Familiar With "Kimi No Na Wa?"

	Heard almost all (All 3 sections)*		Roughly (2 sections)		Partly (1 section)		Not at All (None)		Total
	On Radio	In Movie	On Radio	In Movie	On Radio	In Movie	On Radio	In Movie	
Unmarried	5	4	2	5	5	4	1	0	13
Married	3	3	8	2	1	1	0	6	12
Total	8	7	10	7	6	5	1	6	25

* The movie "Kimi No Na Wa" was divided and shown in three sections.

Table II

How did you feel about "Kimi No Na Wa" as you heard it on the radio? As you saw it in the movie?

	Very Good		Good		Poor		Bad		Total	
	Radio	Movie	Radio	Movie	Radio	Movie	Radio	Movie	Radio	Movie
Unmarried women	3	1	9	2	1	7	0	3	13	13
Married women	5	2	4	2	3	2	0	0	12	6
Total	8	3	13	4	4	9	0	3	25	19

Table III
Attitudes Toward Haruki

	Favorable	Favorable-Critical	Critical
Unmarried women	4	5	4
Married women	7	3	2

Table IV
Attitudes Toward Machiko

	Favorable	Favorable-Critical	Critical
Unmarried women	1	6	6
Married women	7	2	3

CULTURAL ASPECTS OF
JAPANESE GIRLS' OPERA

by Mamory Mochizuki

"What is "Girls' Opera?" Quite obviously it is opera performed by girls. Yet you will find that girls' opera is different from what you expect due partly to the social characteristics of Japanese girls, and partly to the characteristic transformation produced by a foreign culture.

First of all, you might imagine that girls' opera is designed to attract male audiences. Exactly the opposite; girls' opera is entertainment for girls, by girls, and about girls. You can find a few males in the audiences, but they are either fathers accompanying their daughters, or men motivated by strange curiosity. Very few men will accept an invitation to girls' opera.

The girls' opera is "opera" in the sense that there is a story and the girls sing accompanied by an orchestra. However, it is in no way like Verdi, Weber, or Puccini. It includes elements derived from musical shows, Kabuki, and Noh plays. In other words, girls' opera is a mixture of Western and Japanese elements. And in the mixing process, each element has lost its original form. In a sense, the girls' opera popularizes these different arts; it transforms them so that teen-age girls can understand them; it takes seriousness and eroticism out of their original form and makes them harmless.

Now what was the origin of girls' opera? To answer this question, let me paraphrase an excerpt from a "Forty Year History of Girls' Opera," published in 1955. In the center of Japan's main island Honshu, lies Osaka, the second largest city in Japan. The Japanese are fond of hotspring resorts and there was none near Osaka. In 1892 an artificial "hot" spring was made at Takarazuka, 10 miles west of Osaka, from cold mineral springs. The railroad company became interested in establishing entertainment facilities at the spa to stimulate passenger traffic. First they built an indoor swimming pool, but this failed to acquire popularity. Next they organized a girls' chorus to perform in the swimming pool building.

This idea was new because usually the main attraction of a spa is Geisha entertainment. However, the idea was very successful. In 1914, a girls' chorus of twenty members first performed opera on the stage in the former swimming pool building at Takarazuka. Some dancing scenes were included, and there was orchestral accompaniment. The lyrics and music were composed with a view to making them suitable for young singers and dancers. This enterprise initiated by I. Kobayashi, the president of the railroad company, succeeded in attracting people to the spa. In 1918, the opera group performed in the Imperial Theater in Tokyo and achieved moderate success.

At the same time, the "Takarazuka School of Music and Opera" for the training of the girls, was established and accredited by the Minister of Education. Kobayashi was the Director.

Thus, the members of the girls' opera became students, and even now, their performances are planned on the basis of their schoolwork. Since they were schoolgirls themselves, they could become "friends" of all Japanese girl students. Thus girls' opera entered a new phase.

By the early 1920's Takarazuka was famous not for its spa but for its opera, and many girls visited to see the performances. Adults and males attended rarely in this period.

In 1924 a new Takarazuka Girls' Opera House was completed. The new theater had 4,000 seats, and the enterprise developed rapidly. Meanwhile, stimulated by the success of the girls' opera, another group was organized in Tokyo sponsored by a local theater management.

The school and the railroad company made a tremendous effort to make the opera more pleasant and attractive. A staff member was dispatched to Europe and America to learn special production techniques. One result was the performance, in 1936-38 of shows on a relatively large scale. The titles (which were in English) reflected a definite American influence: for example, "Manhattan Rhythm," "Hawaii-New York," and "Big Apple."

In 1933, the school was commissioned as a friendship mission to Germany and Italy and they performed in those countries. Another group, at the same time, visited the United States and performed in the San Francisco Opera House and several other places. These overseas performances, however, were not successful.

The girls' opera was increasingly directed to the needs of the military during the 1930's, and a group of the members were sent to China to entertain the troops in 1934. The entertainment tours continued throughout the war. At home, they were permitted only to perform operas based on Japanese traditional arts. However, this wartime restriction did not cut the audiences, because the fans were more interested in their favorite stars than in the repertory. Therefore, in spite of war, girls' opera continued to prosper.

In 1944, in accordance with the "Regulation of Luxurious Entertainment" the opera was closed, and the theaters were converted to factories for parachutes and other military necessities. The stars were sent to factories, military camps, hospitals, and other places to perform "policy entertainment."

After the war, the Occupation forces were very strict in their censorship of Kabuki and other theater arts because of their revenge themes. But they were more lenient with the girls' opera, and in 1946 the Takarazuka Opera was reopened (with the adjective "girls'" omitted). Their first program was an adaptation of Bizet's *Carmen,* which had not been permitted during the war. During this period both performers and audiences suffered from shortages of all kinds. (It was said that one star appeared on the stage having eaten only a piece of potato.) However, within a few years, they were back at the same level of prosperity which they had enjoyed before the war.

THE FUNCTION OF GIRLS' OPERA

Before and during the war the girls' opera was essentially a product of the traditional social system in which women were restricted. Attendance at the opera was the only outlet for the social interests of young girls which was acceptable to parents and teachers. Dating and other expressions of interest in boys were not permitted. The only social contact these girls had with "males" was with the girl actresses on the stage acting the roles of boys. Girls' opera was viewed as harmless from the standpoint of the rigid national social policy.

This was illustrated by the organization of the Opera School itself. The students were confined in a dormitory, and they were forbidden to meet boys. Called "virgins in uniform", their dormitory was called "a prison without lattices."

But this social attitude began to change after the war. Japanese girls became aware of themselves, and manifested a desire for greater freedom and mobility. Like their audiences, the stars of the girls' opera wished to be independent. They refused any longer to live in a special circumscribed culture of their own, and the management could not stem the trend.

One of the stars who deserted the old opera group was

Koshiji Fubuki. The management was surprised when she announced that she wished to play on other stages and to be treated as an adult. However, the public generally felt that it was a matter for her own decision. Thanks partly to her talent and personality, and partly to the interest of the general public in seeing how a "Takarazuka girl" would get along in the adult world, she turned out to be a success after resigning from the girls' opera group.

Now that the democratization of girls has spread through coeducation and the postwar educational system, the interest in girls' opera has declined, and the dedicated fans are in the minority.

THE RELATIONSHIP BETWEEN STARS AND FANS

Measured by the size of its audiences and the vastness of its stage, it is true that the girls' opera is one of the major theatrical arts. But it has always been handicapped because it is performed by girls for girls. This limiting factor detracts from its status as art. In spite of severe criticism by journalists, the management seems to think "anything is all right that is all right with the audience; besides, this is not a serious business."

The reason why girls alone make up the audience at the girls' opera can be understood in terms of the social characteristics of Japanese girls. Although the situation has recently changed somewhat, average middle class parents protect their daughters from boys. They want their girls to have a happy marriage, and because they wish her happiness, they seek a husband for her themselves. Frequently, parents are more enthusiastic about looking for a boy than is the girl herself. When they find a groom they show his picture to the girls, and later they introduce the boy to the girl. In this kind of arrangement, the parents' judgment is regarded as far sounder than the daughter's, and thus sometimes parents arrange a marriage against the girl's will. In this way girls are protected.

However, the parents think that because of the family system the girl cannot possibly be happier after marriage than she is at home, even if her in-laws are extremely generous and the groom extremely nice. So they indulge her with freedom in her own family until she leaves to become a member of another family. It is a fact that married women in Japan, especially those with children, have no spare time even to go to the movies. Thus, the parents think, "We'll let our daughter be free to see movies and to enjoy herself while she is ours, as long as these things are harmless." For parents like these, girls' opera is the most suitable form of entertainment for their daughters. In the case of Kabuki there have been scandals between handsome actors and upper-class ladies which lead parents to regard the Kabuki and similar entertainment as dangerous for young girls. But the girls' opera is safe and innocuous.

Parents do not mind if their daughters become fans of stars in the opera, because such infatuation is directed toward someone of the same sex, and will not stain her virgin purity. Occasionally, because of homosexual tendencies, some fans do not wish to marry or show other abnormal behavior, but Japanese parents are wise enough to know that this kind of thing is temporary and they ignore the girl's behavior. In other words, they regard it as something like the measles, a childhood disorder, which will soon pass away.

The opera company is aware of the situation and emphasizes to the audience that, "Stars are students of singing and dancing. You too are high school students, aren't you? You must study hard like the stars do." In other words, they argue that the relationship between stars and fans should be that of good friendship among school girls.

It is difficult to describe the behavior of the fans. They shout the names of their favorite stars when they appear on the stage. The design and the color of stars' dresses are soon imitated. "A friendship society with so-and-so" is oragnized among the fans of a particular star. Fans feel satisfaction in touching the dress or shoes of the star. Some stars are fortunate to live in dormitories where visitors are restricted, for if they were free to live in their own homes, their private lives would be destroyed by enthusiastic fans.

In one sense, this situation is similar to that of the American teen-age craze over popular male singing stars, but in the case of girls' opera fans, their enthusiasm is directed toward the same sex and the stars are connected with the girls' opera institution. In Japan, too, fans are satisfied to see their favorite stars on the stage, regardless of the quality of their performance.

Some stars marry, but most pass their marriageable age. As long as they are unmarried, they are still referred to as girls, though they are usually a little older than their fans. This is important because fans look up to their idols as older sisters. Aside from the ones who get married, many stars open shop when they finish their stage careers. They sell accessories, dolls, and other commodities of interest to young women and they rely on their old fans as good customers. Sometimes they manage a type of snack-bar featuring light food keyed to the taste of young girls. The food tastes of the fans are quite standardized. Just as the girls' opera is harmless, this food is light enough to protect a girl from overeating. When an old star manages this kind of shop, old fans will be profitable customers. It is necessary for stars to open such shops on retirement because otherwise, even with the savings of ten or fifteen years of stage life, it is difficult to get along. They are not well paid while they are stars because they are treated not as real artists, but as students. Since a student is at best a semi-amateur, the management feels justified in paying them low wages. This is one reason why Koshiji resigned to become an independent movie and radio star.

Before the war school girls were strictly prohibited from having boy friends, and this caused platonic homosexual relationships among them. The relationship between stars and fans of the girls' opera has a similar background, with this same homosexual tendency. In a homosexual relation, there is usually a strong admiration for an older girl on the part of a younger one; there was rarely a reciprocation of this feeling on the part of the older girl, i.e., the star.

After the war, with the adoption of coeducation, this homosexual tendency has been rapidly disappearing, and the general attitude of the fans has also changed considerably. However, a few fans today show a stronger homosexual orientation than did prewar fans, because girls who are basically uninterested in boys cannot find in a coeducational school an outlet for their homosexual interests, and consequently they become more extreme fans than ever.

Among girl students, those who aspire to go to college have less interest in girls' opera than those who do not. Those who desire further education are less preoccupied with the period between school and marriage which is the basis of girls' opera culture. The fans are, in most cases, those girls who think that they should marry a man whom their parents choose for them after they graduate from high school, and become good wives and clever mothers. The family background of most of these fans, then, is still traditionalistic, though the fans sometimes assume the appearance of bad girls.

A star should be an unmarried girl. If she gets married, she cannot be a star, because as is clear from our discussion, the star-fan relationship is based on a latent homosexual interest. The degree of the fans' enthusiasm depends on whether a star appears on the stage dressed as a boy or as a girl. Generally, the most popular stars are those who take boys' rôles. The most popular star, who has maintained her popularity over a long period, is Takiko Mizunoe (usually called "Tarky"). When she appears on the stage wearing a tuxedo with a rose in her lapel, her eyebrows brushed very dark, singing in a low voice, the fans react with great excitement, just as American girls over Frank Sinatra. Once a girl gets married, she very quickly loses this enthusiasm and stops this type of behavior altogether.

THE CONTENT OF GIRLS' OPERA

One of the principal characteristics of girls' opera as a whole is its use of fantasy, although the content of individual programs is widely varied. The theme of love, for instance, is usually treated in an unrealistic fashion, and most frequently the stage is set in exotic and unfamiliar locales. Paris, New York, Hawaii, Arabia, and India are the favorite scenes of the stories. When Japan is the setting for a love story it is treated as a fantasy which took place long years ago in the feudal period. The characters and costumes are kept unfamiliar to contemporary Japanese audiences.

Thus the girls' opera is escapist entertainment with fantastic, exotic, and romantic content. Japanese women, especially unmarried women, seek such escape since for centuries they have felt no control over their own happiness; their lives have been controlled by an outside fate beyond their ability to change. In such a situation, an individual tends to escape into daydreams, and the girls' opera provided an outlet for this need. That, however, may in part be changing.

PROSPECTS FOR THE FUTURE OF GIRLS' OPERA

The degree of excitement of the true fans seems to have changed relatively little, dspite the changes that have taken place in society. The nature of this excitement and enthusiasm has, however, changed considerably. Formerly the fans sought escape in the theater, but contemporary fans are becoming more realistic and are looking to the stage for lessons in popularity and success.

In 1954 the Tokyo Takarazuka Theater, which had been used by the Occupation forces for ten years, was returned to its original owner, and the girls' opera is once again as prosperóus as ever. Perhaps the girls' opera may in time develop into a real musical show or opera, thereby attracting both young men and women in its audience, and at the same time making a richer contribution to Japanese culture.

A CONTENT ANALYSIS OF "YAKUZA" FICTION: The Way of Life of Kunisada Chuji*

by Muchitaro Tada

In his book, *Popular Ideals in the Tokugawa Period,*** Tokoku Kitamura said:

> The Yakuza is the first ideal which the people of Japan built for themselves by themselves. It is not sound to define it as vulgar. The culture of a nation can find its own values only when the vulgar class, which has been despised, creates its own ideals. It is true that the ideal of Yakuza is not healthy, but it will be the suicide of Japanese culture if we crush all the ideals of the Japanese and sow the seeds of Western civilization instead.

---

* First published in the *Me* magazine, March 1953. The author is a specialist in French literature and also interested in communication problems.

"Yakuza" refers to professional gamblers in the 18th and early 19th centuries. According to historians, they were generally bandits who exploited farmers by violence. However, in popular fiction they are described as Robin Hood-type heroic thieves. Though they disappeared after the Meiji Restoration, stories about them are among the most popular fiction.

In a sense Yakuza stories are an equivalent of Westerns in America, with such themes as violence, lawlessness, protection of the weak.

Kunisada Chuji, whom Mr. Tada uses as a case study, is one of the most famous Yakuza bosses, appearing frequently in fiction, movies, and drama.

** *Tokugawashi jidai no heiminteki Riso,* 1892. The Tokugawa Period was the last stage of Japanese feudalism, 1600-1867.

I was moved and aroused when I first read this book. We have discussed heroes and heroines of Western novels, but never Kunisada Chuji, the hero of the most popular Japanese literature. We have been wrong to disregard our own ideals. Our culture can develop only when we face up to our own tradition and, if it is distorted, struggle with its defects.

If we criticize our traditions on the basis of imported thought which we regard as more valuable, and if that leads to the disorganization of our traditions, it means the over-all destruction of Japanese culture. In order to revive our own tradition, we have to criticize it not from the outside but from the inside.

Yakuza literature presents what Mr. Kitamura called the first traditional ideal created by the Japanese people. This paper is a general treatment of Kunisada Chuji, the most famous Yakuza to appear in fiction.*

A BRIEF SUMMARY OF THE STORY OF KUNISADA CHUJI **

Kunisada Chuji (1810-1850) was born the son of poor peasants in Tochigi Prefecture. He started his career as a pack-horse driver, but after his mother was killed he became a gambler and sought to destroy the evil in his community.

Through his genius at gambling he made a great deal of money and became a boss in his village. He had many able followers and never hurt good people in the community. He distributed money he earned to poor peasants

---

* He was an actual Yakuza in the Tochigi Prefecture.
** There are several editions of this story. The story was originally told with simple stringed instrument (Naniwa bushi), and oral narration (Kodan).
  Written stories of Kunisada Chuji are, more or less, based upon stenographic editions of these narrations. The quotations herein were made from "Kunisada Chuji" by Shun Hasegawa, 1935, and "Kyokaku Kunisada Chuji" of the Kodan Kenkyu-kai edition.

and so came to be respected by the farmers as a living Buddha.

To expand his territory, he attacked the bosses in other communities and became the "great boss" of the whole prefecture. He was accused of murder by local officers, but was never arrested. He also attacked the local governor who was cruel to the peasants.

Together with his followers, he fought his way past an interprefectural barrier, killing some officers. Pursued by the police for this crime, he retreated to Mount Akagi. Lacking food on the mountain he dismissed his group, called the "Kunisada Family." Then alone and disguised he went on a journey, helping the poor and attacking the rich.

At last, sick and unable to move, he was found by the police and punished by death.

Kunisada Chuji, we note, was originally a very common man. He was neither hero, nor mighty warrior. Though trained in fencing by a Samurai called Nakagawa Yuzo, he never finished his course. His only distinction was his genius at gambling, which showed even when fifteen years old.

Though born in a very poor farmer's family, he was ambitious for fame and for recognition as a man. This personality would be familiar to anyone who lived at the end of the Tokugawa Period, and who lived at the bottom of the society.

Chuji succeeded in his ambition. At last he won evaluation by society as: "Chuji is a wonderful guy. His clothes are not good, but he is spectacular, and he is an absolutely great boss."

How could he win this high evaluation? Unlike Miyamoto Musashi,* he had no opportunity to train himself through contact with great men like Zeami or Koetsu. The son of a poor peasant cannot know such cultured

* See the article on "The Content Analysis of Miyamoto Musashi" in this volume.

men.* Musashi was the son of a country gentleman. Nor was Chuji interested in metaphysical ideas like the "Path of Truth" or "Nothingness," about which Musashi was eager to learn. He became a famous Yakuza in a quite different way from Musashi.

For him, the only way to polish the man was either gambling or fighting. A Samurai (feudal retainer) has his own norms called Bushido or "the way of the warrior." A rich man can develop his personality through business. But what of a peasant, confined in a family, digging the soil all the time? He can create his own ideas only when he moulds his future, his social activity, his isolation by his own will and judgment. A poor peasant could participate in dramatic social activities only through agrarian revolt (Ikki)** or in a Yakuza group.

Throughout the story, Kunisada Chuji involves himself in fighting. Sometimes it was unavoidable, and sometimes meaningless. Such fights served both for his training and for tension reduction.

How did fighting serve for training? When a man is in a sword fight, he concentrates all of his past experiences on one point, and engages in purposive behavior with all the power of his will. A man who through his own judgment and will power has experienced this intensive moment, will behave with more self-confidence and surer judgment than before.

What is called "polishing of man", or the "training of man", refers to this process.

But for Chuji, fighting is also an outlet for repressed emotion, and his bloodshed is always rather cruel. In most cases, he initiates the fighting in revenge. He killed Isaburo and attacked the local governor, to exact an eye

---

* The meaning of training and self-discipline in Japanese culture was well discussed by Ruth Benedict. See Chapter 11 of *The Chrysanthemum and the Sword.*
** Ikki means a farmers' riot against the feudal lord. Most Ikki were local, but some became nationwide. The number of Ikki increased during the Tokugawa Period as the feudal economy became disorganized.

for an eye. He was a highly emotional person and became hysterically excited especially when attacking gambling houses. One of his followers, in avenging an injury to his wife, killed his victim by inches (Chuji did not participate in this killing directly). People who read or hear these stories reduce their own frustrations through these cruel passages. This kind of brutality is found throughout much Yakuza fiction. Tengu Gakuzo, a great thief, evaluated Chuji as follows: "Many guys live by the sword in this country, but the spirit of Yakuza is not yet accomplished. Chuji is the man who was born to fulfill it."

What is this spirit of Yakuza, if Chuji created it in bloodshed? First of all, I want to mention several of his less attractive traits, which are not part of the positive spirit of Yakuza.

a) Nonaffectionate: He says openly, "I like women." But he never loved a woman. He has his wife and two mistresses, and he also has relations with innumerable women when he is out of town. However, for him they are merely sexual objects; he relaxes with women. There is no love in him.

b) Crude: He is not an amiable man. Everyone shudders when he sees Chuji's stinging eyes.

c) Unthinking: "Chuji! Don't break away. Sneak by." The enemy wants to catch him, but he cannot understand their strategy. "What? Sneak? Hang it! Tell me who is a sneak." Thus irritated, Chuji lost the battle.

Chuji reveals this lack of foresight not only in each battle but also in more general planning for the future. Chased by the police, he retreats with his followers to Mount Akagi, but there is no reason for choosing that mountain. Soon shortage of food on the mountain compells him to dismiss his group.

These three traits are weaknesses of Chuji, not of the spirit of Yakuza. What, then, are the elements which make up this spirit:

The ideal of Yakuza is, first of all, to keep face.* A Yakuza must behave in a way in keeping with his public reputation. To know shame** is another important virtue for Yakuza. Chuji's economic principle was domestic frugality and public generosity. By so acting, he was able to expand his territory and be considered by the people as a "man among men." Also, to accord with the norms of Yakuza, when expanding his territory, he had to do it by force.

To expand and hold this area, the following virtues were necessary:

a) Boldness: Even in the most critical situation, Chuji fears nothing. "Boss, don't you care about the footsteps outside?" "Yes I do, of course," Chuji replied. "But you don't move even an inch," "Why? I am boss. Can I be afraid of the footsteps?"

Several times he lost battles; he was emotional but never afraid.

b) Affection for followers: Once, when he was in a crisis with followers he said, "I don't care if I die, but I want to save these two boys somehow." To keep and love good followers is one of the most important virtues of a boss.

c) Generosity: His household finances were sometimes strained but he never let that be known to his followers.***

He once attacked Risaburo, an evil man, and took money from him, "But Chuji was not a man to spend money on himself. Instead of drinking and gambling, he distributed the money among peasants in the community."

d) Humility before the honest: As a group, though aggressive against authority, Yakuza respect and help the

* For the Japanese concept of "face," see Weston La Barr, "Some Observations on Character Structure in the Orient: The Japanese," *Psychiatry*, VIII 3, pp. 319-342.
** See Ruth Benedict, *op. cit.*, Chapter 8.
*** The followers usually lived in the boss's house and were boarded by him.

honest or common man. Chuji ordered his followers, "Don't hurt or quarrel with the honest." This code was strict and involved severe punishment of followers who failed to keep it. There was another order saying, "Help the honest in their difficulties," and a follower who could not do this was despised.

Originally, Chuji took it for granted that "gambling is the business of the outcaste," and he could not be proud of his occupation. But, he said, "We gamblers will do the things which no others can do, and pay back the community. We will help the peasants in their misery." He tried various things: he swept blackmailers from the village, he stole money from a rich family and distributed it to the villagers, and he planned irrigation works for the farmers. However, he was unable to analyze the reasons for the peasants' misery. He lacked insight, and consequently his behavior is full of contradictions. Once he said, "Even on the highway, I have never walked past an honest man.* By doing this, I want to earn a reputation among the people and prosper."

The Yakuza's *raison d'etre* is to help the honest and by doing so to increase his own fame. This is a contradiction.

Chuji's outlook on his life is essentially nihilistic. He can feel his own value only when fighting in the midst of blood. He fights for fighting's sake and gambles his own life. He fights in revenge, but what he is really seeking is the thrill and tension he can find only in fighting. He expresses ennui when he has retreated: "'I want to do something, which nobody can do but Chuji!' A follower asked, 'Boss, do you have any idea?' Chuji replied, 'Idea? If I did, I wouldn't be thinking right here.'"

His nihilism is more clearly conveyed in Hasegawa's than in other texts, but in all of them, that which leads Chuji from one episode to the next is the power of dark nihilism. This power, I believe, has been deep in the

---

* It is regarded as impolite to overtake and pass a person on the street.

Japanese people from the Tokugawa Period up to the present.

APPENDIX:
CHARACTERISTICS OF JAPANESE QUARRELS

The Yakuza is sometimes also called a "professional fighter." Therefore, Yakuza cannot be understood without considering the characteristics of Japanese quarrels in general. The following is a summary of the characteristics of Japanese patterns of quarreling, as reviewed in the articles published in the *Shiso no Kagaku*, June 1954, special issue for the study of quarrels.

The Japanese pattern of quarreling is, first of all, emotional. It lacks an orientation to problem solving. The purpose of a quarrel is mostly to feel refreshed, rather than to eliminate the basis of frustration. Frequently, then, it is natural to forget the original reason for the quarrel and fight just in order to reduce accumulated frustrations. (Michio Nagai, "Quarrels in Japan".)

In children's quarrels in European countries the following seem to be the rules:

1) Retort promptly: The first counterattack takes place as a verbal retort. The retort should make a point embarrassing the opponent.

2) Do not take initiative in fighting: It is wise to be cautious; it is wrong to attack first. Don't fire until fired upon.

3) Fight face to face: The worst thing is to attack from the rear.

4) Do not be emotional: A boy should always be calm and not excited.

5) Defeat does not mean dishonor: Mothers expect their sons to be defeated in a fair fight rather than to win by wrong tactics.

By contrast, among Japanese children, there are several different rules, though some are shared in common with children in Europe:

182

1) A prompt retort is not expected in Japan. The worst thing for children is to speak loudly.

2) It is wise to take the initiative in attack, rather than to counterattack.

3) It is not desirable to attack the opponent from the back, but at the same time to be attacked from the back means a lack of caution.

4) To get overexcited is not thought to be good, but it is also not desirable to be completely calm and unexcited.

5) Japanese mothers expect of their children only that they win a fight. There are mothers who will give a club to a boy who has once lost a fight, saying, "You cannot come home until you win!" This last point, in my opinion, is the most important characteristic of the Japanese quarrel. (Kanji Hatano, "Children's Quarrels.")

A Yakuza group is composed of experts in fighting. The following are the factors which are necessary to win a fight.

Individual factors:
1) Physical ability and skill in fencing.
2) Boldness.
3) To take the initiative in an attack.
4) Eloquent blustering.
5) Planned strategy.

Group factors:
1) Good followers.
2) To secure the way for retreat. This is especially necessary when Yakuza fight government officers.

A CONTENT ANALYSIS OF *MIYAMOTO MUSASHI*, A POPULAR NOVEL*

by The Group for the
Study of Popular Culture **

I. SUMMARY OF THE STORY

Two young soldiers were found among the remnants of
the Toyotomi army after the famous battle of Sekigahara
(early 17th century).   One was Matahachi and the other
was Musashi.   They came from the same village, and after
the battle they retreated together.   But Matahachi, who
lacked will power, was seduced by a woman along the
way.   Musashi came back alone to his village to see his
elder sister and Otsu, the fiancée of Matahachi.

---

* Japanese knighthood, or *Bushido,* has been one of the key
moral norms of the Samurai caste who ruled feudal Japan.   The
spirit of knighthood not only survives in contemporary Japan but
is also admired, though less consciously, by the people.

A remarkable genre of Japanese popular fiction consists of
historical stories describing noble Samurai deeds.   Among such his-
torical stories, the most popular may be *Miyamoto Musashi* by Eiji
Yoshikawa; the story of an artistic, self-trained, and brave Samurai.
This work is worth sociological investigation because its circula-
(Continued on Next Page)

** The group was organized at the Institute of Humanistic
Sciences, Kyoto University.   The members are: Kinichi Higuchi,
Fujioka, Takeo Kuwabara, Michitaro Tada, Shunsuke Tsurumi, Tadao
Umesao.   This article was translated from the *Shiso* magazine,
January 1953.

Musashi was disappointed at the changes that had taken place in the village during his absence. Enemy officers were on the watch in the village for any remnants of the Toyotomi army. Osugi, Matahachi's mother, thought that her son had been ruined because of Musashi. Disillusioned, he tended toward nihilism and became destructive. But at this critical juncture Takuan, a priest, taught Musashi that the purpose of every human being is to pursue the truth. Musashi was moved by the words of the priest and began his journey to seek the truth.

Immediately, two women started in pursuit of Musashi. One was Osugi, who wanted to kill him because of her son, and the other was Otsu who, deserted by her fiancée, Matahachi, found herself attracted by Musashi.

After several years of severe training on the trip, Musashi appeared in Kyoto, the capital of the country, in order to test himself. He went to the Yoshioka School of fencing, the most famous of the day, and challenged Yoshioka and his followers. In the duel Musashi defeated the school completely. Thus the name of Musashi became famous.

At the same time, Musashi visited many fencers and learned the essentials of fencing discipline. He also became acquainted with artists and tried to be a warrior who knew both bravery and arts, especially the spirit of compassion (Mononoaware).

While in Kyoto, he met with Kojiro Sasaki, a young and arrogant fencing genius, who thereafter became his lifetime competitor.

---

tion is very great among people in all social strata. A readership survey made prior to this content analysis revealed that this ten-volume novel conveyed a *Weltanschauung* to its readers. The author of the story is skilful enough to relate each event to contemporary problems, and readers are seeking formulas for problem-solving in their daily lives. So the term "historical" is only a partial description of the significance of the story.

Musashi became famous through the novel written by Mr. Yoshikawa. Not only books but also movies, drama, and story telling have appeared based on his text. Thus Musashi has become one of the most popular figures in Japanese popular fiction. He was a strong fencer and an earnest thinker about human life.

Musashi then went to Yedo (Tokyo) for further training, but to avoid the crucial competition with Kojiro, who incidentally came to the same school, he retired for a while into the country, where he took to the plough instead of the sword. In the village he repulsed the attacks of brigands and taught the villagers self-government and self defense.

Meanwhile, the opportunity arose for Musashi, on the recommendation of many well-known fencers, to become fencing instructor to the Shogun (the ruler of Japan), but because of Kojiro's slanders, Musashi was turned down. However, he was not downhearted. Taking his misfortune as further discipline from heaven, he continued to work and study hard.

About this time he had reached an impasse in his training which he could not break through; he felt a wall to stand in his way. But then he met a Buddhist priest, Gudo, who taught him the solution to his worries. The solution was the philosophy that in this world he could rely on nothing but himself. This was the ultimate he could reach in his training.

The time had come to meet his competitor, Kojiro, in duel. By then Kojiro had, with genius, defeated many famous fencers and become instructor to a feudal lord.

The day before the duel, which was held on a small island in the Inland Sea, Musashi accidentally met Otsu who loved him and Osugi who now regretted her hostility.

Musashi won his duel on Funashima island, now a famous incident in popular legend. But although Musashi killed Kojiro, the sword of Kojiro also nicked Musashi slightly on the head. The significance of this duel was that the sword of spiritual training won over the sword of mere technique and strength. The mediocre man who trained himself with toil and effort, won over a man of talent satisfied with his own endowment.

II. SIGNIFICANCE OF THE STORY

"I have many things on my mind to discuss with you whom I regard as my teacher and consultant. There are few books in this confused society that can encourage us young men. But Miyamoto Musashi does teach us how to live and can encourage us." (Excerpt from a letter sent to the author of *Miyamoto Musashi.*)

This is the kind of expectation with which hundreds and thousands of readers read the ten volumes of *Miyamoto Musashi,* looking for instruction for their lives.

"If we can have the spirit of Musashi, defeat in war will mean nothing to us. I assert that the reconstruction of Japan must start from the spirit of Musashi."

"It will be easy to reconstruct a cultural nation if we follow even in small measure Musashi's way of life."

Miyamoto Musashi is read both as a source of encouragement for a defeated people and as a basis of reconstructing a "cultural nation" which has been the slogan of the post-war Japanese government. The image of Musashi has had a strong influence on such men as Furuhashi (the great swimmer), Kimura (the chess champion), and even on the Chief of the National Police. These well-known people are readers of the story and get something out of it. Why has this long story been so popular before, during, and after the war?

III. METHOD OF ANALYSIS

In order to find the answers to these questions we must examine the text. However, scrutinizing the text cannot reveal the meaning actually conveyed, but only a bundle of possibilities that "This passage *can be* read in this way." A meaning becomes a meaning only when a text is actually read by someone. Thus, as the pre-test for a content analysis, we needed case studies to find how various elements of the text were actually read. For this purpose we first made a small interview study, exploring readers' interpretations of the text* and on the basis of that have now proceded to a symbolic analysis.

In the preliminary study, we listed the reactions which this work aroused among a few readers. In the present study we prepared cards on which items related to these reactions are recorded identifying the place and mode of their appearance in the book. In this content analysis, each passage of the text was coded as "Person A appears as having idea *a*." For instance, p. 91 of Vol. X is registered on a card as "Musashi (Obligation to society)."

Five of us took two volumes each to code. To avoid misinterpretation through the individual ideosyncrasies of coders, we discussed the passages likely to be misinterpreted. The quotations in this article are limited to those passages whose interpretation was agreed to by all the authors: We used the postwar edition of *Miyamoto Musashi* (1949-50) as our text.

The purpose of this study is to reconstruct the image of Miyamoto Musashi. It is our belief that this analysis will provide clues to problems of Japanese culture.

IV. MUSASHI'S VALUES: 1) SELF-DISCIPLINE

"The sword alone!"
"This is the only thing on which I can rely."
Musashi touched his hand to his sword.
"I shall live by it! I shall regard this sword as my soul and see how far I can reach! Takuan is doing his training in Zen (a Buddhist sect). I will do it through the sword. I must polish myself even more highly than he." (Vol. I, p. 265)

When he started his new life at the age of 21, "he walked strongly. His eyes were full of hope and youth." (I. 265) But self-discipline is not an easy road. Later he said:

"I am still immature, imperfect, and I cannot reach the real essentials. The more I walk, the longer the way I must go. I feel that I am walking on an endless mountain." (VIII. 34)

Musashi can never forget discipline. He is always looking

---

* "A Tentative Study of Popular Fiction," *Shiso,* August 1951. See the Appendix of this article.

for training. The personality of Musashi is, above all, characterized by a *discipline-compulsion.*

> "An old mother is good to have. I wish I had mine."
> Musashi was attacked by lonely sadness and thought over the life he was going to live. He had lost his parents already. His only sister was living alone in his home village which does not accept him.
> He bent his head quietly for awhile. He spent only three days at this inn.
> "Now I shall leave."
> He took his favorite sword and buckled it on his tight waist. At this moment his strong will-power overcame his sadness. His mind turned to his pledge to regard the sword as parents, wife, and brothers. (V. 71)

He wanted the affection of kin, but his desire was frustrated by the indifference of his villagers when he returned from battle. Even when he visited his uncle and aunt in Kyoto, they treated him coldly—more coldly than an ordinary man. Musashi could enjoy family love like other people. He unconsciously expected this affection from people, but always experienced bitter frustration.

> "I still have the impulse to rely on relatives. I have always warned myself to be self-reliant and alone. But still I rely on others. ...Foolish and incautious, I am not perfect yet." (IV. 12)

He thus suppressed his ordinary craving for family affection in order not to be disappointed. Family affection, he maintained is for common men, not for the Samurai. However, since he was living in society, he had to find some principle other than kinship by which he could achieve ties with others. The principle should be independent of human individuals, so that it would not frustrate him. This principle was termed by him "Michi" (the path of truth). When he could separate Michi from familial affection, he was more or less relaxed.

However, he could not suppress rival principles completely. Sometimes he experienced severe conflicts between principles. Several times his system of values became unsteady. However, at least in his mind his own principle became dominant. Moreover, his resolve to serve both sword and art was generalized into higher metaphysical ideas.

> "However long I stare at it, a circle is always a circle. Endless, eternal, and indifferent, a circle. If it is extended into space, it makes heaven and earth; if condensed, it is the existence of myself.
>
> "The self is a circle, the cosmos also is a circle. They cannot be different things. Both are identical." (X, 15)

It is worth noting that this metaphysical mood is treated as of the highest value in this novel. Musashi's discipline-compulsion resulted in this philosophical personality, and this was the very factor which won for him the duel at Funashima Island.

> "How did I win?"
> "Was it technique or heaven's help?"
> He could deny both definitely. But he could not understand just what his power was. It was something beyond technique or heaven's help. Kojiro believed in the sword of technique and strength, while Musashi believed in the sword of spirit. That was the sole difference. (X, 273)

Musashi, who pledged himself to the philosophy of self-reliance demanded the same of others. The degrees to which they possessed it was Musashi's criterion for evaluating them. Invited to tea once, he reflected, "In this difficult world, people are painting pictures and serving tea.... These people live in a world different from mine, people of leisure, with inherited property," (IV, 134) and he sought to excuse himself to return home. But when the tea was served, he was impressed by the manner, and impressed by the tea cup made by Koetsu. (IV, 155) He re-evaluated them. For Musashi, painting and sculpture are tasks devoted to the "path of truth." But his concept of "path of truth," based on his discipline-compulsion, could not comprehend the values of the rich content of the life of a non-compulsive cultured man. Musashi's personality was simple, and he did not know how to enjoy life. Yoshinodayu, an expert on enjoyment, gave him lessons in relaxation, even breaking her favorite strings to do so, but Musashi could feel such enjoyment only for three days of vacation. (V, 74)

Now it is clear that his concept of "path of truth" does not have any theoretical content. His "path" was, actually, based on the culture of the ruling class of the day. He was obedient to the feudal lords. (IX, 28; X, 198) His ideal of "the governing of the earth" by the sword in fact expressed this attitude toward the established social order, though he rejected ordinary personal contact with upper class people.

Musashi's "path" overlapped considerably with the knighthood of the day, and consequently it was an acceptable pattern. However, while ordinary men sought kinship as well as more formal relations and regarded them both as complementary, Musashi regarded these two principles as incompatible. This assumption is the basic theme of his discipline-compulsion. Therefore, no human affection softens his hard search for the "path".

> "So tell her that, for a man in training, reunion is of no profit. I must overcome difficulties, look for pain, and throw myself into the valley of hardship. Unless I do so, I cannot catch the light. . . . This is the only way to become a real warrior." (V, 107)

He scolds himself for his lack of financial ability, (VII, 77) or feels ashamed of himself when he is cheated by men (VI, 135). He encourages Matahachi, saying, "After you overcome a bitter difficulty you feel a pleasure greater than the difficulty. In human life, pleasure comes after pain. If you want to live in one of them alone, there is no meaning in life." (IX, 256)

Musashi's "path" continues thus endlessly.

We may now summarize his system of ideas on discipline. The following passages make the essential points.

> " . . . Nature is great only when it is seen by human beings. God exists only when He can communicate to a human mind. Therefore, human beings are the creatures who make the greatest achievements and acts. Moreover, a human being is a living creature."
>
> " . . . Man is not far from God and the universe." (VI, 80)
>
> "The sword should always be the path. ...I will seek how a petty individual can melt into nature and feel security in it. I do not know whether it can be attained or not, but I will try as far as I can. My aim is to accomplish this idea. I will go on until I can identify the sword with the path." (VI, 125)

Musashi changed his concept of the sword after he experienced the cultivation of fields in a village. He was more eager to teach the farmers how to govern the community than to teach fencings to the Shogun. The sword of conquest and killing had already been explored by many fencers. Musashi was thinking of a sword and path which would lead all the rest. Learning, preserving, and polishing." . . . If there be a way of the sword which a man can keep until his death. . . . Isn't it possible to govern society by the sword? Is it impossible to make the people secure?" (VIII, 47)

"I do consider that bravery is not the sole basis of politics. When bravery combines with the arts harmoniously, there exists perfect politics. It also is the ultimate aim of the sword. . . . But for me, immature person that I am, a dream is a dream. Before talking about politics, I must learn many things from the people." (IX, 25)

Finally, we must note that Musashi is frequently described as entering the state of "nothingness." Musashi's discipline seems to develop as he has a series of experiences of "nothingness."

V. MUSASHI'S VALUES: 2) KINSHIP AFFECTION

The author of *Miyamoto Musashi* has said:

In every work I have emphasized the theme of kinship affection. On this theme, I am really blind. I am a fool about it. I am irrational where family love is concerned. . . . Without exception, some kind of family love is involved in all my works. (Interview with Mr. Hattori, *Dokusho Shinbun,* No. 625, 1952.)

Paralleling the author's own testimony, we find in the analysis of the story a theme which may well be called the obligation of *kinship affection.*

"Killing your father? . . . Even if you are thinking of it seriously, you are not a son of a man. Even a boy . . . brought up like a wild rat should instinctively know what parents are. . . . Even animals have the instinct of filial affection." (VI, 330)

Musashi himself reflected on his past and said, "If there had not been my sister, I might have become a very cruel person. I used to obey her every word." (I, 38)

His kinship affection embraced not only siblings and parents but also relatives.

His relatives were few. Musashi thought that he must understand them with good will, and also he wanted to help each throughout his life. (XXIV, 10)

From parents, siblings, and relatives, his affection extended to "Those people of the past who are connected with him by blood." (IV, 323). What was important for him was the blood relationship. His relationship with Matahachi seems to be that of friendship, but Matahachi was a man who came from the same village and not exactly a friend of his.

Musashi's concept of "home province" (IX, 265) is the extension of his family concept. He can feel the same affection both for his parents and for those who came from the same province. We can observe a kind of regionalism in his thought. It contrasts to the Western pattern of the development of affection where kinship extends to friendship and further to the global love of human beings.

Musashi thinks of society as an idealistic extension of his home province. He thinks that if he acts frankly and with sincerity, people will "not treat him badly." He thinks that conflicts take place because people lack training and are not aware of their connectedness with others.

The author of the story once commented on a contemporary student demonstration, "I must deplore the fact that the trouble took place between students and policemen both of whose ancestors are the same." *(The Asahi Weekly,* June 15, 1952.)

Since all people come from the same ancestors, one should be thankful to the society composed of these people. Musashi is strongly obliged to society.* "The fact that I am living is an obligation to society." (X, 91) The ultimate extension of his concept of obligation is Heaven.

"Wonderful New Year. At least Heaven gives everyone a happy New Year. Even I, a humble being, was given a slice of rice cake." ** (VI, 19)

For him, "there is no devil in human society." On every occasion, Musashi is conscious of an "immeasurable obligation to the human world." (IX, 14) At the same

---

* "Obligation" is the translation of *On.*
** Rice cakes for New Year are a customary food, like turkey for Christmas.

time, he must think of repaying this obligation. (Giri)

When he reflects on his past, "he is ashamed of himself" especially before his parents and ancestors.

> Musashi thought that he had disgraced the name of his ancestors. He felt no concern about Terumasa, a feudal lord, but he felt completely ashamed of himself before his ancestors (I, 251)

In his concern with the name of his ancestors we can observe the delicate connection of "On and Giri" (obligation and its repayment) with "Haji" (shame).

> "I am careful about my name, like most Samurai. If I disgrace my family name, I must be ashamed before my ancestors. Above all, I want not to be a man who will be laughed at by the people." (VIII, 3)

In other words, a man who is afraid of being laughed at and who knows "shame" is a man who recognizes his "immeasurable obligation to his ancestors." Any criticism from the public is criticism from his ancestors, parents, and relatives. The latter are all tied to each other by the principle of blood. Musashi's blood is looking at him affectionately, but he will suffer severe sanctions if he is not obedient to it. Musashi is afraid of the sanction as are Japanese people in general. For a country, as for a family, the important thing is concord.

> The important points for a group of retainers are, first their individual personality, and second concord in their interrelationships. (VIII, 285)

Thus by extending familial concepts to the public, Musashi includes in his *Weltanschauung* the Japanese Nation and the Imperial Family.

> Iori [Musashi's disciple] then extended his hands upward, and looked through his fingers. He shouted again.
> "The blood of the sun, the blood of my body, same colour."
> He clapped his hands, and while he worshipped he thought to himself:
> "Monkeys have their parents. I do not. Monkeys have no ancestor-Goddess. I do."
> His mind was full of joy, and he could not hold back his tears. (VIII, 168)

194

The key to Yoshikawa, the author, is not only that he emphasizes kinship affection in all his works "without exception," but also that he extends the concept of kinship affection more and more broadly, finally reaching the ancestor-Goddess.

VI. MUSASHI'S VALUES: 3) PITY

Yoshinodayu once said to Musashi that "Strength is not the only virtue of man." We may summarize the virtues other than bravery and strength, as feelings of pity. Musashi was a brave fencer, but in his later period he became an advocate of the spirit of pity.

At the beginning, Otsu described Musashi:

> "He is a real son of the Samurai! He is pure and faithful, Besides, he is also soft-hearted, naive, and sympathetic." (I, 196)
> Musashi spread his arms and wiped his eyes. Because he was suddenly touched by warm human love, his mind, which had been full of suspicion and anxiety, recalled the human world. (I, 112)

This human feeling is closely related with manly and noble traits. He discussed it as follows:

> " . . . I preserve my life in order to die for the nation, for the sake of knighthood (Bushido), in case of emergency. . . . Keep your life manly and noble and love it." (X, 168)

"Preserving life," in the way Musashi does it, is a virtue, for he does it subject to the aesthetic conditions of being manly and noble. If a man preserves his life except under these conditions, his life should be despised. Only when these conditions are satisfied can preserving life be associated with accomplishing knighthood.

What then is the purpose of accomplishing Bushido (knighthood)? How can Bushido be justified? That was a very difficult philosophical problem for Musashi, as for Yoshikawa. Musashi reached an interesting conclusion. The solution appears in a passage which we may call "The dialogue of Musashi."

> "Even the worst man in the world can be saved by Buddha.

If he is aware of salvation, Buddha will forgive him. . . . That is more true after he dies."

"Then, may I assume that both loyal retainers and bad men will be the same after death?"

"No," he continued strongly. "Do not be so irresponsible. A Samurai respects his name. A Samurai who disgraces his name will never be saved."

"Why, then, did Buddha regard good and bad as the same?"

"Human nature is the same everywhere. But those who are seduced by fame or desire become public enemies and evil men. . . . In his thousands of volumes, Buddha, without hate, urged them to be aware of salvation. But it is more worthwhile to reach this awareness while still living. . . . After death there is nothing."

"I see."

With comprehending expression, Iori suddenly said animatedly:

" . . . But a Samurai is different, isn't he? Something is there even after he is dead. Isn't that right?"

"Why?"

"Because his name will remain."

"Hum!"

"Sometimes bad names, . . . at other times good names."

"Hum!"

"Even after he has become a skeleton."

" . . . But," Musashi added to offset Iori's over-simple interpretation, "But a Samurai must at the same time know the spirit of pity. A Samurai without this spirit is like a wild field without moon or flowers. Bravery alone means no more than a storm. . . . A man who devotes his life to the sword especially needs this attitude."

Iori now is silent. "Silent, . . . and he innocently prayed." (VIII, 125)

A man may be saved by Buddha, but the Samurai have name and shame. The virtue necessary for a Samurai is beyond "the way of the Buddha." Further, "the spirit of pity" goes beyond ordinary knighthood. In a word, the moral value system of Musashi is constructed around pity, name, and Buddha. However, name does not justify Buddha and pity does not justify name. This means that it is wrong to regard this series as a hierarchy. Instead, all of these virtues interpenetrate each other and form a whole.

The importance of a virtue is determined by the degree to which it covers the whole.

The reason pity is regarded as more important than name, and name more than Buddha, is that pity and name cover more of the whole. Furthermore, pity cannot be a substitute for name, because name covers certain parts of the whole not covered by pity.

There is some hierarchical organization of virtues other than those in this series. For instance, pity *includes* soft-heartedness. What, then, is the concept which includes pity? Perhaps it is the feeling of evanescence.

> The body has already been assimilated into soil and grass. It has ceased to be human and is in the phase of wind. . . . The identity of life and death. (II, 138)

Further, what is the concept which covers the feeling of evanescence? (We come to the final point.) The concepts which include it are "Nothingness" and "Path." These concepts are those into which all virtues penetrate.

In passing, it may be noted that there is hardly any Buddhist influence in the feeling of evanescence.

> The sadness after a victory . . . is a secular sentiment of the wise. It is a sentiment which a man in the process of training is not permitted to feel. But, Musashi was wandering in the midst of an endless wild field, in unbearable loneliness. (IV, 125)

This loneliness—the feeling of evanescence—is rather aesthetic than religious and ethical. Indeed, all the pity values in the story are predominantly aesthetic. Moreover, nothingness which is identical with the whole, has an aesthetic meaning rather than its original meaning as used by the Zen school of Buddhism. That may be shown by the fact that in "the dialogue of Musashi," pity is more prevalent than Buddha.

VII. CONCLUSION

In the preceding sections we have analyzed the content of *Miyamoto Musashi* and tried to elucidate the basic themes of the story. However, since some minor items included in each of three series of themes were not mentioned in the discussion, we would like to enumerate here the full contents of the three series of values.

1. Self-discipline values—*Path, nothingness,* obedience to nature, respect for bravery, artistic discipline, will-power, self-reliance, readiness, strategy, importance of life, manliness.

2. Kinship affection values—*Kinship affection,* obligation (*On*), repayment (*Giri*), concord in human relations, obligation to heaven, family name, shame.

3. Pity series—*evanescence,* compassion, tenderness, softheartedness.

All of these themes appear throughout the ten volumes of the story. Here, as a tentative summary, we shall try to give Musashi's answer to the question of how to live. Musashi might have answered with the following statement of "This I Believe":

"There is a law in *nature* and a *path of truth* in the human world. There is no meaning to *life* if a man does not pursue that path but passes his days in idleness. It is easy to master minor techniques both in *swordmanship* and the *arts,* but the manly life can be attained only when a man tries to pursue the ways of arts and swordmanship aiming at the state of *nothingness.* However, bravery is not the only virtue of human beings. Those who lack the feeling of pity cannot be called men. When I observe the human world in its changing phases I am struck by *evanescence* and I cannot restrain my *tears* for the *sadness of things* and for the innocence of the son of man. But, man loves his kin. Evanescence is one phase of *nature* and *blood affection* another phase of natural instincts. Moreover, this affection can be extended to relatives, ancestors, people of the same region, and all human beings in the world. My very existence is indebted to the *kindness of society.* In consideration of this obligation, I must obey the *norms* of society in order *not to disgrace my family name.* It is also important not to disturb *concord in human relations.* These things are identical with *sincerity* before the people's ancestor Goddess. This is the true and natural life for me."

As noted before, it is difficult to systematize the inter-relationships of these ways of living. But, we wish to propose a tentative thesis.

There is no consistency in the interrelationships of these items. In some cases item A justifies item B so that they construct an hierarchy. In other cases item C', C'', all appear as phases of item C. For instance, (Path of truth-nothingness, evanescence, pity, tenderness, soft-hearted-ness), the latter items being in hierarchical order. But among them (Path-nothingness) and (evanescence) are both at the same time phases of nature.

In the sense that all of these items are integrated in Musashi, they are organized as a bundle. However, we cannot say that they are systematically integrated. It would be artificial to try to interpret them as a system like the Christian moral value system. The characteristics of Musashi simply exist ambiguously on the same level, and these fragments compose the whole, which rejects systematic interpretation. This pattern, in fact, is the characteristic mode of existence of Musashi's (and, in a sense, Japanese) virtues.

Now, careful readers may have noticed in Musashi's statement of "This I Believe" that two items were not mentioned. They are self-reliance and readiness-strategy. Why could we not include them in the statement?

The reason in the case of self-reliance is that the concept is used as the switch from the kinship-affection theme to the self-discipline theme. As we mentioned before, he became aware of the need for self-reliance to the extent that he was frustrated in affection. But this does not imply that he denigrated blood affection. His training and path aimed at concord in human relations. Musashi used the principle of self-reliance as the means to reach certain ends: the principle itself is not worthy of respect.

There are many stories in Japanese about severe self-discipline leading a man to fame, and Musashi's concept of self-discipline is closely related to these. *Prima facie,* that seems to be an "establishment of individuality," but unlike Western individualism, the individual himself is not regarded as worthy of respect. In Japanese society, an individual may have his own value only when it is recognized through meek submission in relations with other human beings. In a word, self-reliance is the means to attain higher values. Consequently, Musashi is not an advocate of individuality, though he himself had the problem very much on his mind.

"Readiness" and "strategy" appear in the text several times. But in Japan these items are not supposed to be expressed explicitly, because they involve utilitarian balancing, which is regarded as mean. Note the description of merchants in Yoshikawa's writings: "In this world, foxy is a priest, clever is a merchant, strong is a retainer, ignorant is a noble." (IV, 421) Though merchants are thus described, they appear in the story always as bit players only. Yoshikawa cannot write about merchants whose lives are concentrated on profit-making. This limits Yoshikawa's writings as modern fiction. The limitation may reflect the social culture of contemporary Japan.

As the conclusion of this report, we would like to propose a hypothesis for further study: that the characteristic traits of Miyamoto Musashi and their pattern may be identical with those of the Japanese people.

In the absence of scientific study of the basic personality of the Japanese, this is merely a hypothesis. However, there is the fact that this story is read by many readers for instruction. (See fan letters and results of our previous survey.) Moreover, in considerable degree, the characteristics we found in Musashi are identical with those noted in the studies of Ruth Benedict, Takayoshi Kawashima, and Minory Kida, on Japanese national character.

Our further program is to verify the hypothesis by more extensive studies of readership and to contribute to the study of the basic Japanese moral system.

APPENDIX: A SUMMARY OF THE READER REACTIONS TO MUSASHI*

Needless to say, *Miyamoto Musashi* was one of the most widely read popular stories before, during, and after the war. Before examining the content characteristics of the fiction, we felt it necessary to see how a passage of the text was read by the readers.

We conducted intensive interviews with three readers of the story in the city of Kyoto. Those interviewed were: the master of a small shop, a carpenter, and a Geisha girl. At the same time, we conducted Rorschach tests on these people to check the personality backgrounds of their responses. The questionnaire was flexible.

We found, first of all, that all of them read the story in order to a large extent to get guidance for their lives.

The second finding concerned attitudes toward elements in the story. There were sympathies with a character (for instance, one respondent showed deep sympathy with the hero). There were also sympathies with themes of the book (e.g., one showed sympathy with Musashi's concept of discipline, regardless of, or with very slight attention to, his person). From this pretest we could thus construct a list of items with which readers sympathized or which they rejected.

This audience research brought another by-product. In Japanese society, the correct answer to a specific question is very difficult to obtain by direct questions, but, this study showed that a projective method in terms of people's likes and dislikes regarding popular fiction, movies, etc., will serve as an index of their attitudes.

---

* Published in the *Shiso* magazine, August 1951. This summary was made at the request of the authors.

THREE WAYS OF THINKING IN CONTEMPORARY JAPANESE HISTORY[*]

by Shunsuke Tsurumi

I. INTRODUCTION

Meaning is many-faced. It is like a windmill with several blades. Which blade turns up when the windmill stands still is, to some degree, a matter of chance.

We may classify meaning, following Charles W. Morris[**], in five primary modes, the identificative, the formative, the designative, the appraisive, and the prescriptive and classify signs by the name of the mode of meaning dominant in each. Even then, what is labeled a "designative sign" may have once in its embryonic stage before formulation possessed the possibility of taking shape as an "appraisive sign." For this embryonic stage of a sign in existence, we will give the name an "ur-sign." If a sign is a linguistic expression which is labeled a "prescriptive sign," the ur-sign of this sign may be an inner sign that produced this outward expression. At this antecedent stage as an ur-sign, it is possible that what later turned

[*] Reprinted from *The Science of Thought*, Vol. I, (Tokyo, 1954), pp. 54-63.
[**] C.W. Morris, *Signs, Language and Behavior*, 1946.

out to be a "prescriptive sign" was in a more indeterminate status in regard to the dominant mode of meaning. A set of expressions, "Go away!" (prescriptive), "I desire that you go away." (designative), "Your departure is desirable" (appraisive) may be alternative developments from the same ur-sign before certain factors, some of which are chance factors or factors unrelated to the meaning of the ur-sign, intervened and led to the choice of only one among the possible candidates. The chosen sign, then, stands in a certain relation to those other signs not chosen. The set of these signs are not equivalent in meaning, but they are "transformable" to each other, that is to say, they are replaceable by each other with changes of meaning so slight that the need that gave rise to one sign may be relieved by any of those that belong to the set. Such transformability may hold between signs belonging to different dominant modes of meaning. Following Charles Stevenson's definition of "good,"* we may state that the transformability between "This is good" and "I approve of this" can be raised by modifying the latter to "I approve of this and I want you, too, to approve of this."

This mobile character of meaning which we find in respect to simple signs has its analogue for more complex sign combinations.

Morris has provided a scheme of classification of 16 specialized language types in terms of four modes of signifying (formative, designative, appraisive, and prescriptive) and four kinds of use of signs (systemic, informative, valuative, and incitive). These 16 language types roughly correspond to mathematics, science, fiction, law, cosmology, myth, poetry, morality, criticism, technology, politics, religion, propaganda, rhetoric, grammar, and metaphysics. These specialized languages are by no means tight compartments. When we examine them in concrete historical contexts, we find various transactions between the specializ-

---

* C. L. Stevenson, *Ethics and Language,* 1944.

ed languages. What concerns us here is a corollary of the "transformability" of signs, i.e., the "usurpation" of one special language by another. The Bible, for example, is an instance of the language of religion, that fits into the niche of signs with prescriptive meaning put to incitive use. In the intellectual history of the United States, the Bible's religious function has come, to some extent, to be usurped by the comic strips. Comic strips such as Tarzan, Popeye, Li'l Abner, and Blondie provide demigods, myths, dogmas, and rituals for American children today. The comics being an instance of the language of fiction, we may say that the language of religion has been usurped by the language of fiction in this case.*

In any period of history, convergences and divergences of different genres of communication of thought are continually taking place. Sometimes there is an upheaval that results in a breakdown of many genres of communication and their replacement by new ones. Certain periods may be distinctly marked as periods of radical change in communication. These periods do not exactly correspond to the periods of radical change in politics and economics.**

One who watches these phenomena, elucidates their significance to the public, and works for the improvement of communication may be called a "communication critic." The interdependence of genres of communication requires that communication become an object of unitary grasp and criticism. Great philosophers were often communication critics in this sense. We may recall Plato and Aristotle for the Classical Age, Augustine and Aquinas for the Middle Ages, Leonardo for the Renaissance, Leibnitz and Rousseau for the Modern Age, Dewey and Cassirer among contemporary philosophers.*** Rousseau among them is the ablest

---

* S. Tsurumi, "The History of American Comics," The Sekai Hyoron, 1948.
** Tsurumi, Tada, and Higuchi, "Rousseau in the History of Communication," *Rousseau*, edited by T. Kuwabara, 1951.
*** S. Tsurumi, "Communication," *Studies on Dewey*, edited by K. Tsurumi, 1952.

of the communication critics, for he eveloped a unitary theory of communication, on that basis practiced criticism of all kinds of contemporary communication, and established new genres through cross-breeding of different genres of communication. In contrast to Voltaire, Rousseau's revolutionary philosophy was matched by his equally revolutionary means of communication. It was through his effort that revolutionary thought in 18th-century France was set in interaction with the masses of people.

Such a train of ideas leads us to re-examine the theory of signs in historical perspective. We feel that the system of semiotic nomenclature which owes its genesis to logic needs to be reoriented in terms of the history of communication. Tools forged in analytic philosophy need to be tested in coping with concrete descriptive tasks.

As an example of such a study, we will attempt a brief characterization of the contemporary intellectual situation in Japan in terms of the transactions between different genres in the history of communication. We will see in turn how each genre of communication is related to the character of the thought communicated in this genre and, taken as a whole, how the availability of only a limited number of genres restricts the development of thought for the nation. Development may be possible through learning the principles of the different genres of communication, criticizing one genre of communication in terms of the principles of another, and expanding the possibility of each one of the genres of communication. For this purpose, we need to accumulate concrete case studies in communication criticism.

Communication prepares the conditions for changes in the structure of society, and, in its turn, is influenced by changes in the structure of society. The history of communication is consequently marked by phases of radical change which take place before or after (but not together with) radical changes in social structure. In Japan the period immediately following the Meiji Restoration (1868) is one such transitory period in the domain of communication. At the end of this Post-Restoration period (1890), as we may call it, there emerged a number of prototypes in the realm of communication which remain effective to the present day.

II. THE LANGUAGE OF SCIENCE

The Post-Restoration left in our hands several means of expression, among which the language of science and the language of fiction are to be noted here for their polarity.

In the Post-Restoration Period, the Japanese Government sought to remodel Japan into a *modern power*. As one of the necessary steps it gave strong support to science. Before and during the Restoration science was promoted primarily by local officials, physicians, and other private citizens. Private colleges like Keio and Doshisha were held in high esteem in the earlier years of Meiji. After the Meiji central government was fully established in Tokyo, however, the situation changed. Gradually, toward the end of the Post-Restoration period, the prestige of the private colleges declined and it has since come to be that the best schools are the government-sponsored Imperial Universities and that the best scholars are those on the government payroll.

Japanese scholars derive their prestige not from the learning they supposedly have attained but from being members of the government. This fact accounts for many of the traits that stand out in the behavior patterns of these scholars. The law department of one Imperial University is known to include many scholars who advocate the unconditional abolition of the status system. And yet when they march out of the dining room, they strictly follow the order of court ranks accorded to them. In the literature department of another Imperial University, scholars interrupt their faculty meeting with a remark,

"Let us light cigarettes now." With this signal all the assistant professors leave the room so that the important issues may be discussed by the eldest members alone. The faculty once included a member (Shotaro Yoneda) who came from Eta stock, a group of people who work in leather and, for this reason, somewhat like the Indian untouchables, are considered lower in status than the Japanese people at large. The time came for this instructor to be promoted to professorial rank. When the motion was introduced at the faculty meeting, a professor remarked sharply, "I cannot bear to sit with a colleague from the Eta community." This professor is noted as a liberal for characterizing as mythical the first 600 years recorded in the official history of Japan. The decision finally reached in the faculty meeting was as follows: that the professor of Eta stock would be promoted to full professor's rank but with the proviso that he promise his resignation within a year after his promotion.

These episodes illustrate what we may term the quasi-heterological character of scientific discourse in Japan. An epithet that is designated heterological is one that is not applicable to the epithet itself. The word "dog" is hetero-logical, because "dog" is itself not a dog. The word "word," on the other hand, is autological, because "word" is itself a word. By transferring this usage, from the dimension of semantics to pragmatics we will call a sign "quasi-heterological," when the sign is not applicable to the sign-user. Now Japanese scholars, from Meiji down to the present, have the habit of talking about the necessity of "enlightening," "modernizing," and "democratizing" with the unconscious postulate that they are not part of the object criticized. In this they are true to the spirit of the Post-Restoration officials who stood above the "three classes of people," by virtue of their being closer to the Emperor, the source of all prestige.

When closely examined in regard to form and structure, academic language in Japan is found to be a sub-language of the bureaucratic language. When the language of science was transcribed from Western languages to Japanese in the Post-Restoration period, the pioneers had to coin many new words. And from what mint? Here they had a free choice. The Meiji scholars deliberately disregarded the everyday language of the people and adopted the language of the Samurai officials of the Pre-Restoration era, a language in which new words are coined by combining two Chinese ideographs as a set. Since Chinese ideographs have an abundance of homonyms, the language of science thus remodelled overnight came to be a language incomprehensible to the ear.* Take any high grade academic piece of writing and read it aloud at normal speed: a Japanese college graduate will not be able to take it down accurately. Thus it is that scholars, when they are engaged in academic discussion, resort to another special language, a second academic jargon in which German, French, or English academic languages both in speaking and writing gives the Japanese scholars a mark of superiority over the common people. In a few departments of science, however, the pioneers who undertook the wholesale transcription of scientific terms resorted to more popular methods of wordbuilding. Thus the nomenclatures of botany and mechanics are comparatively free of the bureaucratic language and lend themselves more easily to romanization than do other departments of science.

III.   THE LANGUAGE OF FICTION

In contrast to the language of science the language of fiction has had an altogether different fate. While the language of science has been sponsored by the government, the

---

* "Symposium on the Academic Language in Japan," *The Science of Thought,* Vol. 2, No. 11, 1949.

language of fiction has been out of favor in official quarters.*

The founder of modern fiction in Japan is Futabatei Shimei (1869-1908). Born the son of a country squire, he was sent to Tokyo to study law. His father expected him to become an official of the Meiji Government. The son, however, did not live up to his father's expectations, instead taking to drink, dissipation, and fiction writing. Indignant at the outcome of his son's education, his father disowned him with the curse "kutabattei shimei" ("die, you dog!") which his son slightly modified to "Futabatei Shimei" (which gives the meaning "wandering in four directions under an arbor of sprouting leaves"). Under this pen name the son published his major novels *Floating Clouds* (1887), *Vestiges* (1906), and *Banality* (1907).

In those days fiction was regarded as an immoral indulgence of rich men's sons. While the language of science inherited not only the Chinese ideograph but also the moralistic style of the Confucian scholars of the Tokugawa period, the language of fiction inherited from the erotic story writers of the Tokugawa period something of the spirit of the playboy. The published writing of Japanese scientists (especially in humanistic sciences) is often forced into a moralistic vein, revealing thereby the unconscious postulate that the author is expected to give admonition to the people. The novelist, on the other hand, suffers from the opposite compulsion, to present his ideas from the point of view of an outcast from the community.

The dominant stream of fiction in Japan is the self-novel (ich-roman); that is, a novel in which the author himself is the hero. There are many different styles of self-novels. At one extreme, there is a writer like Takii Kosaku, who writes only what has really happened in his

---

* Sei Ito, *The Method of the Novel,* 1949; S. Tsurumi," The Characteristics of Japanese Thought and Emperor Worship," *Shiso,* June, 1952.

own life. At the other extreme, there is a writer like Dazai Osamu who lived his life in fictional exaggeration.

Dazai was born in 1909, the fourth son of the richest landlord of the Northern Provinces. Throughout the earlier phases of his schooling he was a top-ranking student. After he entered college, however, he began to suffer from the nervous oscillations which are so characteristic of both his writing and his life. Faithfulness to his own vagrant private feelings was the mainspring both of his life and his fiction. Already in childhood, he sensed hypocrisy in the family morality of his own breed and felt he could breathe more freely in the company of servants. The sense of guilt he felt toward his class background led him to participate in the underground activities of the communist movement. At the same time, his sensitivity did not permit him to rest content with the deductive fixity of Marxist philosophy. Nor did he ever write "proletarian literature." The participants in the communist movement then, as now, conceived of themselves as heroes impeccable in conduct and unerring in judgment. To live and work in such an atmosphere was stifling to a man of his temperament. As a revolt against it, the playful side of his character became dominant both in his living and writing. The Sino-Japanese and the Pacific Wars brought a change in his working conditions.

Dazai managed to survive the war years without writing a single war novel, in this respect showing greater resistance than many Marxist writers. He wrote self-novels from the point of view of an unassuming, foolish, common man and regulated his private life on the same orientation. There is not a single page in his voluminous work that sings praise of bloodshed. The end of the Pacific War and the new national fashion of "democratization" again presented a new series of problems to Dazai's temperament. The Japanese intellectuals who had not even in their private feelings resisted autocracy were now vociferously defending liberty and democracy at the top of their voices under

American leadership. This festal atmosphere was too much for him. Dazai began a series of works which marked the third and last phase of his fiction. In these pieces he presented himself as a weak-willed drunkard, a good-for-nothing, an imbecile, an ugly man no woman likes, a man who can never say no to anybody, a bad father who eats cherries at a restaurant just because his children at home would have liked to eat them.

Dazai never wrote a novel without masochistic distortion. What he wrote did not, as in the case of many other writers, serve to free the author himself from his private predicament but exercised a hypnotic influence upon the subsequent course of his life. This can be explained only in terms of Dazai's neurotic personality. Dazai had little discipline in financial matters, suffered from morphine addiction, spent many months in a mental hospital, and attempted a series of impulsive suicides, the last one of which was successful. To the end of his days, he could not rid himself of the conviction that he was betraying his fellow men by leading the life of a good-for-nothing. But it was through holding faithfully to the point of view of a good-for-nothing that Dazai was able to maintain his critical attitude toward the changing atmosphere of Japan throughout the last twenty years.

The language of science is quasi-heterological, passing judgment upon the Japanese people as a whole, but not including the scientists themselves. But the writer of fiction is quasi-autological to an extreme degree, making apologetic monologues and portraying the Japanese people only insofar as they happen to interfere with the life of the author himself, who is an outcast from the community.

Language in which a man may speak on behalf of the people as a member of the people must be sought elsewhere. As a medium of expression for the Japanese common man's philosophy, Manzai, or vaudeville, fills the niche that has been left vacant by more respectable media like science and fiction. Because in the modernization of Japan the status

211

structure of the pre-Restoration society was preserved, the respectable languages like science and fiction were monopolized by the upper-status groups of society and could not become vehicles of expression for under-currents among the ordinary people.

IV. THE LANGUAGE OF VAUDEVILLE

Manzai is a comic dialogue performed in a vaudeville theater. Its history goes back to Tokugawa days when the Manzai pair paid house visits, giving a dance and an appropriate New Year's message.*

Manzai, a male name meaning "ten thousand years of life", is accompanied by a boon companion, Saizo, whose name means "store of wit". Manzai and Saizo make their appearance in quaint kimonos unchanged since Pre-Restoration days. Their trade, however, is not as prosperous. Now, all the money they can scrape together in a year from their performances may give them barely ten days' livelihood.

In contrast to the unenviable plight of the traditional form of Manzai, there arose in Osaka, after 1916, a new type of Manzai which is a comic dialogue in modern clothing on a vaudeville stage. This new Manzai made a bold break with the stilted pattern of the Pre-Restoration Manzai. Since the 1930's the rejuvenated Manzai has gained ascendency over all other genres of the vaudeville arts. It occupies more than 50%, sometimes 80% of all vaudeville performances in urban districts. The spread of radio, which paralleled the development of Japanese military aggression, 1931-1945, favored the establishment of this new genre, for Manzai was well suited to the function of disseminating war reports to the people. Thus what was only a local affair limited to Osaka in the 1910's became a nationally-known genre of popular arts by 1940.

---

* N. Origuchi, *Illuminations on Japanese Literature,* 1950.

The Manzai dialogues consist of rapidly shifting stereotypes which, when not in operation, may be neatly filed. Into these stereotypes are fitted particular episodes, figures, events, and names which happen to be popular at the time. The use of the stereotype is a sure-fire technique in drawing laughs from the audience and for activating patterns of thought which give vent to the under-currents of the common man's philosophy. The stereotypes are freely exchanged among the Manzai artists. If one sits all day long in an unknown local theater listening to ten Manzai couples each giving three performances, one is certain to hear the same gag used several times by different couples.

Manzai teams accept plagiarism with a magnanimity rarely seen in the higher arts. Strictly speaking, there is no plagiarism, for the existing stereotypes, which are natural outgrowth of the basic culture of Japan, are the common property of the community as a whole, including both the Manzai and the audience. The audience will come out of the theater and will, from that moment on, make free use of the same stock of stereotypes in their conversation. What sets the pattern for racy conversation in Japan today is not the theater, not literature, not scholarly lectures, but Manzai. There is an ample stock of stereotypes, each of which, when used appropriately, bears endless repetition. The originality of the Manzai artist (or the Manzai script writer) consists of his skilful combination of the stereotypes. Manzai, like the movies, is an art of montage. In contradistinction to the movies, however, Manzai is extemporaneous. The Manzai player enters backstage and, on the basis of a few minutes' observation of the audience responding to the preceding Manzai couple, decides what stereotypes to use in his next performance.

It is impossible here to give a detailed list of stereotype categories in use. Let us therefore take just a few examples. In correspondence with the jealousy and *Schadenfreude* which operate powerfully in the basic personality in Japan, gags designed to disparage the opponent are often used.

To the man:—"Your honorable scalp has less hair on it than when I saw it last."

To the woman:—"Your legs are shaped like radishes."

To either:—"Your nose is so inconspicuous."

These stereotypes taken together amount to a picture of what the Japanese feel are their greatest physical handicaps.

Let us now turn to the disparagement of the opponent in regard to mental capacity, moral conduct, living standard, and other aspects of life. In each category, there is a representative set of remarks touching on the elements of the inferiority complexes of Japanese life.

The disparagement is never a one-sided affair. In the earliest phase of the dialogue, one of the parties may get the upper hand and put on superior airs. Before the dialogue reaches its end, however, his worthless essence is certain to be stripped bare before the whole audience. With whatever refinements a man may disguise himself, man's essence is anything but noble.

The personality which Manzai attributes to males is apparent in the following:

Woman:—"What do you like best in life?"

Man (wriggling uneasily):—"I like liquor second."

Woman:—"What did you say?"

Man (a little louder):—"Liquor comes second."

Woman (impatiently):—"What do you like *best*, I'm asking you?"

Man (desperately):—"Woman!"

According to Manzai philosophy, man's value system consists of (1) Woman, (2) Liquor, (3) Money, (4) Food—in that order. Big shots may talk big, but they are just trying to hide what they really believe in. The plot of many Manzai pieces centers around the attempt, through the Socratic dialogue, to wring a confession of commonness from the genteel partner.

In spite of the fact that Manzai makes fun of the noble

and the great, its spirit is ultimately free from an inferiority complex. Manzai is a hymn in praise of the common man. The common man is full of faults, he makes many blunders, he is often put to shame. But in spite of it all, he is worthy. He approaches truth through his adventuresome blundering. He may enjoy his life by learning to laugh away his public failures. Such a philosophy, skeptical, lusty, and antibureaucratic, offers a striking contrast to the viewpoint of Japanese scholars. Its belief in commonness is sharply distinct from that of the novelist in the total absence of the masochistic distortions which characterize Japanese self-novels. The difference arises from the fact that the Manzai artists are drawn from lower class city-dwellers, whereas scholars are the descendants of the Samurai-officials and novelists are the idle sons of bourgeois families. Biographical studies of the Manzai couples reveal that they consist of "odds and ends" of people. Each of them started out, not with the object of becoming a Manzai player, but with the high ideal of becoming a singer, dancer, shamisen player, story-teller, Kabuki actor, or specialist in one or another of the established genres of popular art. They went into Manzai only after giving up their original ideals. From this arises the hodge-podge character of Manzai. It goes off into a mimicry of the classical dance, then a snatch of a popular song, then a short scene from an old movie. It is a melange of all the existing genres of popular art in Japan.

The fact that professional Manzai players started out with something other than Manzai in view and later turned off into Manzai is significant. Many genres of popular art, notably the popular novel and the movie, paint pictures of man heroically striving for a high ideal and in the end achieving it. In real life, however, man starts out with a high ideal and then is weaned away from his original inspiration. Men may be classified by the kinds of ideal they start their lives with. Men may also be classified according to the manner in which they are weaned away

215

from their original ideals. To obtain useful knowledge about grown-up men, the latter classification is more important. It is how a man tides over the crisis of "weaning" that determines his worth as a full-fledged member of society. Manzai is the genre of the popular arts that deals with this problem of weaning, and therefore it is more serious about the problems of grown men than other genres. Through Manzai, we are able to come into contact with the healthiest currents of thought in the life of the Japanese people today.

APPENDIX: SOME BASIC STATISTICS OF JAPANESE COMMUNICATION*

I. LITERACY RATE AND USE OF LITERACY

1) Literacy (national total)
   Literate — 97.9%   Illiterate — 2.1%

2) Use of written communication by the Japanese (national average).

Those who do not read mail	7.8%
„ „ „ „ „ newspapers	14.3%
„ „ „ „ „ leaflets	17.3%
„ „ „ „ „ public bulletin board	21.8%
„ „ „ „ „ magazines	28.5%

   Those who do not feel the necessity of
   reading and writing as far as their
   occupations are concerned   32.7%

   (Committee for the Study of Literacy, sponsored by
   Minister of Education, 1948)

---

* The statistical data were assembles by H. Kato in collaboration
with the named research organizations which collected them.

II. NEWSPAPERS

1) Number of publishers of daily newspapers   101

2) National total of newspaper copies circulated daily
Morning papers	20,246,362
Evening papers	13,473,297
Total	33,719,659

3) Population covered by one copy (morning and evening inclusive)
   2.47

4) Average number of copies per household daily
Morning papers	1.22
Evening papers	0.81
Total	2.03

5) How often do you read newspapers? (The question was asked of a sample of the population over fifteen years of age.)
Every day	65%
Once in a while	15%
Not at all	20%

   (July 1955)

6) What part of the newspaper do you read first? What part of newspaper do you read every day?

	First	Every day
Social and cultural	24%	21%
Political	24	13
Local news	12	14
Fiction	10	25
Sports	5	9
Women's section	4	7
Editorial	3	7
Comics	1	4

   (July 1955)

7) How much time do you spend on newspaper reading
   every day?
   Less than 15 minutes   16%
   15 to 30 minutes   36%
   30 to 60 minutes   26%
   More than 60 minutes   · 22%

   (July 1955)

8) Do you think that newspapers tell the truth fairly?

	Male	Female	Total
Completely fair	15.9%	12.4%	14.1%
Generally fair	62.2	52.5	57.1
Not so fair	4.6	3.7	4.2
Unfair	0.5	0.1	0.3
Don't know	7.2	17.2	12.3
No response	9.6	14.1	12.0

(July 1955)

(Items 1-4 by Japan Newspaper Association, 5-7 by the
Asahi newspaper, 8 by the Mainichi newspaper.)

III. RADIO BROADCASTING

1) Number of stations:
   N.H.K. non-commercial, national network with
       local stations   160
   Commercial stations   40

   (1955)

2) The increase of radio sets since 1924:

Year	Number	Coverage of total population
1924	5,455	0.1%
1930	778,928	6.1
1935	2,422,111	17.9
1940	5,668,031	39.2
1945	5,728,086	39.2
1950	9,192,934	55.4
1955	12,897,897	77.6

3) Average daily hours of radio use in Tokyo   4.4 hours

4) Content classification of radio programs

	N.H.K.	Commercial stations
Music	} 29.5% {	35.0%
Entertainment		26.7
News	14.6	15.0
Social and cultural	42.3	17.8
Commercial	00.0	2.9
Sports	13.6	1.3
Others	00.0	2.9

(August 1955)

5) Tuning of radio sets in Tokyo area on a Sunday evening:

N.H.K.   25.2%
Three commercial stations   48.4%

(May 8, 1955, from 7 p.m. to 10 p.m.)

6) Ten most popular programs and their proportion of listeners:

1. Three songs (participation program)   42.1%
2. Rokyoku School (participation program)   41.2
3. Dad is Nice (Serial drama)   38.0
4. Wit School (Quiz)   37.2
5. Burlesque show   35.8
6. Laughter show   35.0
7. Zenigata Heiji (Serial drama)   34.8
8. Old melodies   34.4
9. Madame Chakkari (Comic drama)   33.5
10. Hit Parade   33.3

(November 1955)

(Item 1-4 by N.H.K. and Broadcasters Association, 5 by Dentsu Advertising Agency, and 6 by Radio Tokyo Research Bureau).

IV. MOVIES

1) Number of movie theaters   4,079

2) Population per theater   20,961

3) Annual number of movies produced   350

4) Annual number of foreign movies imported and
    shown   201

5) Rate of movie attendance:
    Total population (A)   Total movie attendance (B)
        83,199,000   483,791,000
    The frequency of annual movie attendance per capita

$$\frac{B}{A} = 5.81$$

                                                              (1954)

6) Total amount spent for movie-going (1955, 6 months,
    Jan. to June):
    Japanese movies   11,857 (million Yen)   73%
    Foreign movies   4,431 (million Yen)   27%
        Total   16,288   100%

7) Number of foreign movies shown in Japan by country
    (1952):
    American   140
    British   13
    French   9
    Italian   6
    German   5
    Soviet Russia   3
    Other European   8
        Total   184

8) The "best five" foreign movies in the post war period by box office take*:

	Title	Date of release
1.	Gone With The Wind	Sept. 1952
2.	Roman Holiday	April 1954
3.	Living Desert	Jan. 1955
4.	Shane	Oct. 1953
5.	The Greatest Show on Earth	April 1953

V. THE ROLE OF VARIOUS MEDIA

How did you know about the Shiun Maru accident?**

Through radio	56%
Through newspaper	27
Personal conversation	4
Both radio and newspaper	9
Other sources	2
Don't know about the accident	2

(The Asahi Newspaper Poll, July 1955)

VI. TELEVISION

1) Date of first television broadcast   Feb. 1953
2) Number of TV stations (Jan. 1956)   5
3) Number of TV sets in use (estimate Jan. 1956) 140,000

(Broadcasters' Association and the Asahi)

---

* All "best ten" foreign movies are American. (Japan Movie Industry Association)
** A shipwreck accident in which many students were drowned. The accident took place in early summer 1955.

222

VII. COMMUNICATION ACTIVITY IN ONE RURAL VILLAGE

1) How frequently do you listen to radio?

	Male	Female
Every day	63%	52%
Occasionally	30	38
Practically never	3	0
No answer	3	10

2) What radio programs do you listen to? Mention as many as you like.

	Male	Female
Entertainment	91%	63%
Weather report	89	63
Popular songs	86	85
Quiz program	62	67
Agricultural	52	49
News	31	15
Radio drama	29	69

3) Those who mentioned "agricultural" programs were asked: Have you ever practiced the information you gathered from agricultural programs?

Yes	62%
No	21
No answer	17

4) How frequently do you go to movies?

Two or three times a year	71.6%
Practically never	12.5
Others (including those who go more than three times)	5.3
No answer	10.7

(The data in this section were supplied by the Society for Agricultural Technology, March 1955. Certain tabulations were done by H. Kato.)